Daughter of the Mountains

A Memoir

Sharon Canfield Dorsey

With contributions by Carl Edward Canfield

High Tide Publications, Inc.
Deltaville, Virginia

High Tide Publications, Inc.
1000 Bland Point Road
Deltaville, Virginia 23043
www.HighTidePublications.com

Ordering Information: Quantity sales. Special discounts are available
on quantity purchases by corporations, associations, and others. For
details, contact the "Special Sales Department" at the address above.

Cover by: Vivien Mann

Printed in the United States of America
ISBN: 978-1945990069

Dedication

I dedicate this book...
to my children, Shannon and Steven,
who grew into responsible, caring adults
who make me proud every day,
to their spouses, A. J. and Amy,
who brought even more love and strength to our family,
and to my grandchildren,
Adaline, Emma and Zachary,
my little rays of sunshine, who keep me smiling.

A plaque hangs on the wall in each of our homes,
with this promise:

Our family is a circle of strength and love.
With every birth and every union, the circle grows.
Every joy shared adds more love.
Every crisis faced together makes the circle stronger.

Daughter of the Mountains

Growing up in the mountains of Appalachia,
it really snowed,
glazing the circling peaks with sparkling white powder
that made children pray for a day off from school,
and mothers cast their grateful eyes skyward
when the yellow bus showed up anyway.

Snowy mornings still conjure images
of my Dad carrying buckets of coal
to fire up the big cooking stove in the kitchen.
The aroma of sizzling bacon and hot biscuits
evokes the chill of icy linoleum under my feet,
as I dashed from beneath a mound of warm quilts
to shiver beside the roaring stove.

When the mountains gave up their icy crown in spring,
crystal clear water gurgled its way down the steep slopes,
to settle in rocky creeks, home to bass and catfish
that would end up on our table,
served with cornbread and ramps, the wild onions
we dug from the deepest, darkest places in the woods,
their secret location passed down,
grandfather to father to son.

My Dad and his brothers were indentured to coal,
the black gold they dug from the bowels of the mountain.
When the wailing sirens signaled a cave-in,
families huddled outside the mine,
waiting to see who the angry mountain had claimed.
The mountains gave and the mountains took away.

At twenty, I packed up my possessions
and my brand new husband,
and I left the mountains, forever, I thought,
only to learn as years went by,
the mountains never really left me.
Like demanding parents, they continue to call me back.

Contents

Chapter 6 Musings From The Edge Of Understanding

Chapter 7 My Seventies Rebellion

Chapter 1

Appalachian Childhood

Beginnings

After my mother, Macil June, died in 2013 at age 89, my daughter, Shannon, and I were going through closets and drawers. In the bottom of a small dresser drawer where Mom kept her best jewelry, we found a packet of faded

letters, tied with a yellowed satin ribbon. My father, Carl, had written them to her when he was twenty-six and working as a coal miner in another county. My mother was sixteen and still in high school.

My grandparents, Bessie and Alvin Kuhl, had forbidden the relationship because of the age difference. But Carl and June were deeply in love. Ignoring parental opposition, they eloped, but kept the marriage a secret. My mother finished her last year of high school, still living at home with her parents. My father continued to work in the mines, saving money so they could get a house of their own.

Macil June Kuhl
Carl Eartman Canfield
Wedding Day, 1940

Beginnings

I remember that day,
the first day you told me you loved me...

We walked beneath the trees, the breeze in our hair.
We sat on a hill and watched a boat in the distance,
pondering its destination,
wishing to go along, somewhere, anywhere, together.

We lay on the grass, side by side,
hands clasped, thighs touching,
and gazed into the curtain of green above us.
We kissed, wishing the day would never end.

We spotted a patch of trees across the lake
and dreamed a cozy cottage there.
Then you looked at your watch and I looked at mine.
Together, we folded up our blanket and our dreams.

We stood, arms entwined,
savoring a last moment of nearness, of peace.
We walked through the trees,
into the real world of school and work.

You waved and drove away.
I wiped away a foolish tear and followed,
missing you already.

A Woman's Place

My mother, Macil June, was an organized woman. Every Monday, no matter what the temperature, she washed clothes in a wringer washer. She filled it with water she had drawn from the well and heated on the stove. She

carried the clothes basket up crude, rocky steps, dug into the steep hill, and hung the shirts, dresses, pants and under-wear on the clothesline. Every two weeks, there would be an extra load of sheets and pillow cases. In winter, the clothes froze solid -- sleeves, legs in strange poses, like headless creatures, hanging on the clothesline. She lugged them back down the hill, stiff as boards, dampened them with warm water and put them back in the basket to be ironed on Tuesday, always Tuesday. She even ironed the sheets and towels.

I remember how red and chapped her hands would get from the icy wind. At night, before she went to bed, I would see her coating them with Vaseline. I remember as a small child, offering to kiss them and make them better, the way she always kissed our bumps and bruises.

Wednesday and Thursday were cleaning days. She polished the furniture, mopped the linoleum, did mending and sewing. Friday was baking day, in preparation for the week-end. There was no dessert with supper on week-days, and usually no candy at all, except at Easter and Christmas.

Saturday, when my Dad wasn't working, we drove to town in his rusty pick-up truck to shop in the dime store, buy a few grocery staples, or purchase something from the hardware store. Haircuts were done at home, and, unfortunately, not always well. My brothers often wound up with that "bowl over the head" look. I grew my hair long, and ran when I spotted scissors coming my way. My Mom didn't drive, so she looked forward to the week-ends and a chance to get out of the house. Sunday was Sunday School for my brothers and me in the mornings and a big dinner at noon, with fried chicken or pork chops, mashed potatoes, gravy, green beans and hot biscuits. In garden season, there was tomato, cucumber and green onion salad with vinegar dressing. On summer afternoons, my Dad often drove us to the cemetery to take flowers from the garden to place on the family graves. On the way home, we would drop-in and visit with aunts, uncles, and cousins. There was always more food, and sweet tea. Southern hospitality dictates that you offer food the moment a guest steps in the door.

Sometimes, if the weather was warm, Mom would pack up the fried chicken with potato salad, deviled eggs and pineapple upside-down cake, and we would drive out for a picnic. Dad always chose the place to stop and eat. He was so picky, we would sometimes drive all afternoon, and wind up back home to picnic on the front porch. Mom would fume, but the man at the wheel was in control. We stopped when he was satisfied with the spot. It was late 40's--early 50's, the era of, "a man is the king of his castle, and women were there to serve."

Our summer vacation was always a camping trip. The coal mines would close for two weeks, beginning with the 4th of July holiday. Miner families, including us, packed up tents, cots, and cooking utensils, and headed for the state park. If money was really scarce and we couldn't afford the $1 a day camping fee, we'd camp near the park, along the river. Mom would work for days, packing and loading the car. We fished and swam during the day with our cousins and friends, roasted marshmallows, and told ghost stories around the campfire at night. It was the high point of our summer.

Black Gold

Daddy was a coal miner, so that meant financial ups and downs; mostly downs. The mining company was the only large employer in the area. There were often strikes over pay or working conditions, which resulted in no

money at all. The mine owners ran a Company Store, that was a large department store where the miners could buy groceries and other necessities on credit. Each miner carried a tab, and the money owed was taken out of his monthly paycheck. The prices at the store were so high that most families never got out of debt. It was a form of slavery. We were poor, but everyone around us was too, so, as kids, it didn't matter to us.

I loved school, and looked forward every year to that first day, waiting for the bus in my brand new school clothes. In August, Mom would get out the Sears & Roebuck Catalogue and let me choose my new clothes. There were, however, very specific guidelines. I was allowed to choose three dresses, two skirts and two sweaters from the $1.50 - 2.96 page. Those would be supplemented by hand-me-downs from older cousins. I would always peep at the prettier, more expensive dresses on the $5.96 page and wish. When the big Sears box arrived on the doorstep, I was a happy girl. It would be many years before an affordable department store would be built in Rainelle, the closest town to us.

Being poor didn't mean being hungry. There was always plenty of food. We planted a big garden and canned or pickled vegetables all summer. Some years, we raised chickens and pigs to butcher for winter. On butchering day,

I would run inside and hide with pillows over my ears so I wouldn't hear the shrieking of the chickens as they were rounded up and carried from the pen to the chopping block. Daddy hunted and fished in the summer and fall. Everything from turtles to deer wound up on our table.

My Aunt Kay had several cows so we always had fresh milk for making butter and cottage cheese. My mother baked cornbread or biscuits for every meal because white bread from the grocery store was too expensive at nineteen cents a loaf, so it was a rare treat. There was a government surplus food program for the poor at that time, and we were eligible. It provided cheese, canned beef, and sometimes butter.

When I was in high school and Daddy would go to sign up for the surplus food, I remember feeling ashamed. By then, I had friends whose parents were not miners, had more money, and lived in nicer houses. Like most teenagers, I didn't like being different from my friends. One of the worst tongue-lashings I ever received from my Dad was the day I begged him not to sign up for the free food. I never asked again. Looking back, I can see my embarrassment hurt him deeply.

I roll my eyes when I hear people wishing for the return of the "good old days." I suspect those people never lived in a house with no indoor plumbing. We had an outhouse behind the house for daytime and warm nights. There was a white, enamel "slop jar" on the enclosed back porch for cold weather. When we were young, my mother had the dubious job of emptying it into the outhouse every morning and scrubbing it with Clorox. As my brothers and I got older, we took turns climbing the hill with the heavy pot. I always dreaded my turn.

The well was also on the back porch. We pulled the water from the well with a pulley attached to a long, slender bucket. It was poured into a smaller, white enamel bucket which sat on a shelf by the door between the back porch and kitchen. There was a metal dipper in the bucket, and we all drank from it. The water was cold, and sweet, and tasted nothing like the stuff that pours from our faucets today. I don't recall being sick often. I guess we built strong immune systems.

Mom mixed cod liver oil in orange juice and forced it down us daily. I still have a strong impulse to hold my nose when I drink orange juice.

Bathing without indoor plumbing was complicated. Mom heated water in the big teakettle on top of the black, iron cook stove in the kitchen. A curtain was hung between the kitchen and the dining room, and we took turns bathing in a round metal tub in front of the stove in the kitchen. It was cozy and warm, and a Saturday night ritual, whether we needed it or not. On week-nights, we scrubbed in the wash basin on the back porch.

Daddy bathed every day because he came home from the mines covered in black coal dust. It lingered in the wrinkles under his eyes, even after he bathed. Unfortunately, it also lingered in his lungs, causing a pulmonary disease which miners call Black Lung.

Coal mining was, and still is, a dangerous profession. Cave-ins were common, and we all feared the whistle that could be heard for miles, announcing an accident.

All the men who lived near-by would run to the mine in case they needed help with rescue. Sometimes, entire families would go and wait anxiously at the mouth of the mine. My Dad was never trapped in a cave-in but we lost many friends. I still remember how my stomach turned over the night the mine supervisor came to tell us that my Uncle Earl had been severely injured in a cave-in. It left him crippled for life. My Dad suffered from a variety of work-related illnesses when he passed away in 1974 at age sixty-one.

My Father's Hands

My father loved to get his hands in the dirt.
He looked forward to spring and planting time,
that specific day decreed by the Farmer's Almanac.
Potato planting came first,
the plow eating through the black earth,
carving out rows of trenches for seed potatoes,
saved from last year's harvest and carefully cut,
making sure each piece had an *eye*
from which a new potato would sprout and grow.
Dad would go down the rows,
covering the pieces gently with his big, calloused hands,
like a blessing of anticipation and appreciation.

Corn planting was next.
A handful of corn kernels, a walk down the plowed rows,
carefully spaced to allow walking room between the rows
and an equal amount of sunshine for each corn stalk.
When the corn was ripe in mid-summer,
we would strip the ears from their stalks,
remove the husks, cut the corn from the cobs
and stuff the kernels into glass canning jars for winter,
but not before roasting some of the fattest ears,
drenching them in butter and gorging.

When green beans were ripe for picking,
Mom and I would sit in the porch swing,
and string bushels of tender beans,
breaking them into canning-sized pieces.
Their bright green jars would join the yellow jars of corn
on sturdy cellar shelves.

We would drag the tall, heavy, ceramic jar
from its cool, cellar corner,
fill it with beans and salty pickling brine
and cover it with muslin cloth.
In late fall, we'd remove the pickled beans, fill more jars,
and add them to the larder.

Tomatoes were a summer delicacy,
ripening to coincide with the 4th of July picnic--
tender baby lettuce, sweet tomatoes,
mayonnaise on venison burgers -- a treat.
When tomato vines produced more fruit than we could eat,
they too, were canned or juiced.
Between summer garden crops, we picked apples,
scoured the woods for blackberries or raspberries,
and concocted a colorful assortment of sinfully sweet jellies
and jams to top Moms fat biscuits.

Thanksgiving would find the cellar filled
with burlap bags of potatoes and crunchy apples,
rainbow-hued jars of vegetables and fruits,
and a freezer full of meat and fish
from Dad's hunting and fishing expeditions.

My dad dug coal in the mines when there was work,
but his real love was tilling the soil.
Home was a simple frame house,
heated by a pot-bellied stove,
with a bucket well on the back porch,
an outhouse on the hill behind.
We didn't have much money,
but my father's hands kept us fed and warm.

9

A Surprise...My Dad, The Poet

I never knew my Dad was a poet. I knew he was the first married man drafted from our little town of Charmco during World War II and how devastating that was to my mother. But I don't recall hearing him talk about those days. I found this poem in my mother's papers after her death. The misspellings are those of a man who left school at an early age to go to work to help support his family. The thoughts are those of a patriot who loved his country.

Old and blemished and flecked with gray
        A forgoten soldier stands
He is dreaming of another day
        He is dreaming of another day
When he served in no mans land
        T was then he held the flying speed
As off A prerrie wind
        A modle of our noable youth
A terrew to berline
                - * -

But every since the world begain
        The march of father time
Has spared not man nor even beast
        But has pasted on and on sublime
Henth bended a score of years
        This brave old warrow stands
He can toil no more in mite of wore
        But he prays for thoes who can
                - * -

Now hark with trimbling lips he speeks
        There is cold scorn in his words
A fleck of pride lights up his cheeks
        And ill his rath he curbs
O hittler not for all your gold
        Or all your stolen lands
Would I betray my strs and strips
        Or betray my fellow man
                - * -

Would while able to draw a breth or pull
        Or pull a triger strate
Sell out the comwards that I loved
        Who died for fredom sake

And the judgment some day
        Let me here thair marching feet
If this request be granted me
        T is a soldier complett/

West Virginia Winter

Maybe it's my imagination, but it seems to me that winters were longer and snowier when I was a child. It was exciting to be the one who made the first footprints in the fresh powder, but my Dad usually had that dubious honor. He was up at dawn, carrying buckets of coal to feed the pot-bellied stove in the living room, and the big cooking stove in the kitchen.

Shivering, my brothers and I would gather around the table, with its red-checkered oilcloth, to devour breakfasts of home-cured bacon or ham, fried eggs from our chickens, and biscuits dripping with butter and blackberry jam. Those were pre-cholesterol-awareness days. We'd wash it all down with tall glasses of cold, sweet milk, fresh from my Aunt Kay's cow.

Sharon June Canfield
Homer Dale Canfield
Snow of 1949

Then we'd begin the lengthy process of bundling up for school. By the way, school didn't close when it snowed. I envied my brothers, whose corduroy pants covered their long underwear and hid it from ridiculing eyes. I hated the woolen snow pants my mother made me wear under my dress. I harbored secret dreams of losing them in the cloakroom, or drying them too close to the stove, and watching them go up in smoke. Once, I actually ditched them in the little bus shelter, and went on to school without them. My plan to put them back on after school, before walking home, back-fired. They were frozen solid. When I sheepishly walked in, carrying the icy lump, my mother didn't say a word. She thawed the snow pants by the stove, dried them out and made me wear them the next day.

When we were all bundled into our coats, wool scarves, gloves, and rubber boots, Mom would stand at the front door and issue brown bag lunches of potted meat sandwiches, crunchy oatmeal cookies, and crisp, red apples. We picked the apples in the fall, and stored them in the cellar, so they would stay fresh all winter.

Mom would hustle us out the door with warnings to "be careful," and "don't skate on the edge of the road." We lived beside a busy highway. In the early morning, large coal trucks passed by on their way to the mines. She knew we liked skating along the edge instead of wading the knee or waist high snow drifts left by the road scrapers. Like stuffed pandas, we'd clump our way to the bus stop, where we'd roughhouse with a half dozen other rubber-booted kids. The bus was always late when it snowed and by the time it arrived, our noses were cherry red, and our fingers and toes tingled. There was an all-out dash to get to the head of the line and stomping as we fought our way up the steps.

The school bus was seldom warmer than the outside, so the real thawing-out process didn't begin until we got to the schoolhouse, and discarded the layers of woolens in the cloakroom. A steamy, pungent odor would fill the room as damp children began to dry out. When I was in the third grade, the pot-bellied stove was replaced by a coal furnace, but somehow that winter odor lingered on.

I still sometimes detect a strangely familiar aroma when I walk into a winter classroom of woolen-clad eight-year-olds, and I can almost taste the potted meat sandwiches, and the oatmeal cookies.

The Cloak Room

It's 7:30 on a snowy mountain morning.
The yellow school bus disgorges it's unruly mob.
My three-grade classroom is a humming beehive.
The airless cloak room fills with familiar smells...

wet woolen snow pants
new rubber boots
potted meat sandwiches.

The noise level in the tiny room crescendos...

crinkling brown paper lunch bags stacking on shelves,
rattling buckles of snow boots lining up in untidy rows,
giggling as we jockey for the coat hook with our name on it.

Then the pushing, shoving escape to the classroom,
and the battle for the best spot around the pot-bellied stove.

Happiness was...

School Days

Throughout the ages, writers have begun their poems and prose with the phrase, "A long, long time ago." I begin my story in the same way. Sixty years ago, a lapboard, tar-papered structure that was Charmco Graded School welcomed me to the first grade, as it had welcomed my siblings, Sharon and Homer, and my mother, Macil June. A vacant shell of that building still stands on U. S. Route 60 in Greenbrier County, West Virginia, a ghostly reminder of a simpler time. The trees that used to shelter the school from the highway are gone, as is the flagpole, where the American flag waved proudly.

A thriving business now occupies what was once grassy space where we played dodge-ball, basketball, and held on tight to the wooden seats of the merry-go-round as the older kids sent us spinning around and around until our heads were spinning too. Countless recesses and lunch breaks were spent taking turns on the nearby swings and slide.

Student Body of Charmco Graded School, 1929
Macil June Kuhl, 1st grade (5th from R, front row)

Visible from the playground was the entrance to a partial basement that housed the coal furnace that provided warmth to a building devoid of modern insulation or thermal windows. In my mother's and sister's days there, heat was provided by a pot-bellied coal stove. The janitors used this underground space as their headquarters, and would occasionally allow a persistent few students to gaze into the open furnace door at the fire-breathing beast that occupied the cavern beneath the classrooms. The grandfatherly janitors looked out for us, and made sure we only looked, and never touched, the red hot surface of the furnace door.

Upstairs, there were classrooms, a closet that doubled as bookstore and candy store during recesses, and two bathrooms. At some point, as a rite of passage, every younger boy got shoved into the girl's bathroom by an older boy, only to discover it was no different from the boy's, except for the absence of urinals lining the outside wall, and it smelled better. Marble tournaments took place on the white concrete floor just outside the bathroom door, making the traditional shoving of the younger students into the forbidden bathroom, very easy.

At that time, school principals didn't sit in their offices. Mr. Meadows, our principal, also taught fifth and sixth grades. It seemed he was everywhere at once. He was on the ballfield. He was in the trees bordering the playground, making wooden whistles for everyone in the springtime when the sap was flowing. He brought gallons of sassafras tea from home for recess and lunch. He was a strict disciplinarian who also tenderly carried hurt and sick students to doctors, or to the homes of grateful parents. He told stories and tall tales with a country drawl that was immediately recognizable. He was the epitome of early educational excellence. He is still a revered, active member of our community. How appropriate that he became Charmco Graded School's last principal. The school closed a short time after I moved on to junior high.

Attached to the original school building was a large room that was once a CCC (Civilian Conservation Corps) barracks. At the end of this room was a stage that rose above the classroom floor two or three steps, with a curtain that opened when there was a Christmas play, Easter program, or other special event. An old upright piano sat silent in one corner of the stage, coming to life when the county music teacher came for a visit. The doors at the rear of the stage opened into the lunchroom. Pine walls with green and white painted rafters framed the tables and chairs that lined each side of the room. A pot-bellied stove warmed the space.

Each school day, this room filled with the aroma of freshly baked rolls or cornbread that accompanied hearty meals of pinto beans with boiled potatoes, fish sticks with French fries, or spaghetti with green salad.

There were peach and pear halves in a sweet syrup, peanut butter and jelly sandwiches, and tomato soup. Tomato soup and grilled cheese sandwich days were my favorite. Fresh baked rolls day was everyone' s favorite.

As we entered the lunch room, the line formed on the left. Crates of milk and, sometimes, ice cream cups, greeted us as we gathered our silverware, trays, and napkins. The trays and bowls were of heavy plastic in pastel colors of green, blue, yellow and pink. The boys would try to get blue or green, avoiding the girly pink bowls. School cooks filled our trays as we moved along the cafeteria serving line, and out the opposing door into the lunchroom. Friends sat with friends, and grades clustered together. Older students who were kitchen helpers carried lunch trays to first graders in their classrooms. Those helpers received a free lunch. The rest of us paid twenty-five cents a day.

My older sister and brother had moved on to junior high and high school by this time, making Charmco Graded School my domain. I would frequently hear, "You are just like your brother", or "Why can't you be more like your sister?" My face would turn bright red as my anger grew. There was no shortage of discipline, even in first grade. My teacher once smacked my hand with a wooden ruler because I had scribbled all over the outline of a duck with a fat crayon instead of coloring within the lines as I was instructed. I thought the scribbles wouldn't show because the crayon was white. She thought differently. In this special place, I received my first kiss, met my future wife, and got paddled a number of times.

I grew to love Charmco Graded School after more than my share of active resistance to school routine. The principal made it his personal quest to deliver me to school in his green pick-up truck several days in a row, until this reluctant third grader got the message that staying at home on a school day was not an option.

That, ironically, was the same year I became a coveted King of the School Carnival. I sat on my throne with my Queen, Karen, on the big stage, as my family and the community looked on. I was so proud in my white shirt and tie and a freshly cut flat top of flaming red hair. The next morning' s newspaper reported the event with our picture and an accompanying story. A copy of that story is on the following page. What a day!

Silence filled those rooms and hallways in the mid-1960's. The flag came down and the entrance bell stopped ringing.

A few years ago, I returned to that place by the side of the road that had been the source of so many fond childhood memories. A sale was being held to empty a storehouse of furniture, antiques, and items from the old school. I left there with the bell that had called the school to order for so many

17

years. I also purchased the chalkboard that had once listed the daily menu in the lunchroom and the pull-down maps from my classroom. These things symbolize for me a time of innocence and joy.

Now I occasionally sit in an old teacher's chair from one of those classrooms of long ago, pondering my own life as I reach an age I once thought reserved for those teachers. Much gratitude is owed to those who were a part of the humble beginnings of so many of us, in a place that felt so safe, in a time that was so uncomplicated.

- Carl Edward Canfield

Charmco King And Queen

Karen McMann, daughter of Mr. and Mrs. Clifford Mc Mann, and Carl Canfield, son of Mr. and Mrs. Carl Canfield, all of Charmco, were crowned king and queen of Charmco School Friday night. The crowning featured the parent teacher association. carnival. Both the king and queen are third grade students.

Carl Edward Canfield
3rd Grade

Coal Country... In Living Color

I have lived my entire life in the small rural community of Charmco, in the southeastern part of West Virginia's coal country. Charmco is one of a half dozen tiny communities in an eight square mile area that sprung up around the mines. Most of them are connected by State Route 60. Houses line that route, facing on the highway with either woods or rivers behind. Driving through, it seems like one continuous community until you see the signs for the individual towns.

My life here has connected me to a number of unique individuals. I still see them in living color, coming and going through my life, touching my heart in positive and, sometimes, negative ways.

My Dad brought many of these colorful characters into our lives in the mid and late 1950's. I think he attracted them because he fit that pattern himself. He was a teller of tall tales and a prankster with the ability to pull gullible people into his realm of fantasy and half-truths. He mined coal most of his life and his co-workers were neighbors, friends, and occasionally, adversaries. The miners shared rides to work, hunted, and fished together, shopped in the same stores, frequented the same gas stations, and went to the same churches. When a mine tragedy struck, it was always someone we knew. One day, we got news that Dad's friend, Withrow, had been caught in the teeth of a continuous mining machine and killed. I had never seen my Dad cry as he did that day. The whole community mourned.

I'm the youngest of three siblings. There's an eight-year difference between the me and my older sister, Sharon. My brother, Homer, who we lost in 2015, was the middle child. By the time I was growing up, Dad had been forced to stop working in the mines. The years of digging in low coal, which required working in a constantly stooped position, combined with his military disabilities, had taken their toll. The last day he worked in the mines, his ride dropped him off at the bottom of the driveway, as usual. I was waiting for him. My mother had to help him up the hill to the house. After that, he worked at odd jobs to pay the bills until he was granted his Social Security benefits, and his veterans disability at age fifty-one. It took a long time to win those bureaucratic battles. In the meantime, life was a struggle, but we never went hungry, and he always provided a comfortable home. During those years after he retired, I was his shadow when I wasn't in school-running errands with him, visiting his friends, or just hanging out in town. Each small business owner in Charmco had a distinct personality, some kind, some scary to a small boy.

The Gas Station...took care of all things car related-gas, oil, repairs. I liked going there with my Dad and watching the hydraulic lift carry the cars up to the ceiling. Jack, the pleasant, young owner, also sold ice cream, Popsicles, and soda. It was a center of activity, and I felt grown-up, hanging out there with my Dad and his buddies.

The Post Office...was across the street. The postmaster was tall and balding, with a gruff voice and intimidating presence that always scared me, even after I learned he was a pastor of one of the local churches. Over the years, I did learn his bark was a little worse than his bite.

The Corner Grocer...wasn't much better. He had zero patience with children, especially me, and I dreaded the days when Dad would send me in to pick up his orders. I used to wonder if he was mean to all the kids, or if he just disliked redheads. Occasionally, his wife would be at the check-out, and her warm smile was a welcome change.

The Produce And Meat Market...was on the other corner of the block, and it was the scariest place of all. The proprietor always had tobacco juice running down his chin from the Mail Pouch tobacco he chewed, and blood covering his white apron from the butchering. He looked like your most feared horror movie villain, and had a disposition to match. As a young teen, I would ride my bike there to use the pay phone, just outside his window. He would scowl at me or yell that my time was up. It was the only phone booth in town, and I braved his wrath to call my girlfriends. Our phone at home was on a short cord in the living room, provided no privacy, and much teasing.

Earl's Tv And Repair Shop...was close by. Earl wore oversized, thick glasses that made his eyes look like baseballs. If our television died, he came to the house and switched out tubes until he found the one that made Jackie Gleason or Lucy reappear on the screen in their fuzzy, black and white grandeur.

On Saturdays, when our family drove the four miles to Rainelle to shop, I would often wait in the car and people watch. There was always a blind man with severe burn scars, playing guitar in front of Murphy's Five and Dime. Nearby, an amputee sat on a rolling platform and sold pencils. A mentally challenged, crippled man wandered through the store, selling the Grit newspaper. These people were much-loved fixtures in the community. Friends stopped to talk with each of them, and give them change. Money was scarce, but everyone tried to give something.

Occasionally, an organ grinder with a monkey on a leash would come to town. The man cranked out music, and the monkey collected coins from the crowd, putting them in an apron around his waist. He wore a tiny straw hat which he tipped to people who gave him money. For weeks after the organ grinder came to town, I begged my Dad for a monkey of my own.

Canfield Brothers
l to r: Earl, Claude, and Carl

My Uncle Virgil owned a barbershop in Rainelle. When we were old enough to balk at Dad's hair-cuts, my brother, Homer, and I would wait our turn for an empty chair and eavesdrop on the conversations. It was entertaining, even if we didn't always understand the gossip.

Televisions were still rare in the 50's. Reception was affected by the weather and the black and white pictures were snowy, at best. Neighbors who couldn't afford televisions of their own, often came to watch their favorite shows with us. Harry and his wife lived across the road, two houses down and came often. He was an Italian immigrant who came to America as a stone mason to work in the mines. His English was still unintelligible to me after many years in the states, but Dad could understand him. Mom opened all the doors and windows after their visits because they reeked of garlic and unwashed bodies. Harry somehow got a driver's license in his 70's and came home with a 1957 Ford Fair Lane. I lusted for that powerful V8. On his first outing, he revved the engine, throwing gravel everywhere, and spun out of his driveway into oncoming traffic. He survived, but the car didn't. I grieved when it was hauled away. The insurance company paid for another car, a 1958 Ford this time, that met its demise in a similar accident a few weeks later. That ended Harry's driving career. From then on, Dad became his transportation.

Harry's gardening was better than his driving, and his huge, red strawberries were famous. In summer, he sold produce in the front yard but, locals knew not to buy it. Harry's fertilizer came from his outdoor toilet.

Our across-the-road neighbors were Luke and Belle. Luke was a kind, skinny scarecrow of a man who looked eight feet tall to me as a child. Belle loved kids, and passed out cookies and cakes to us. Luke drove a small, dark-colored Studebaker that he parked in an old, wooden garage. He came home one day with a new, bright turquoise Studebaker replacement that he attempted to squeeze into the old garage. He got the front of it in, but he couldn't open the car door to get out. Within days, the old garage was gone, and the new Studebaker parked proudly in the driveway for all to admire.

I loved looking across the road at Christmas time to see the tall spruce in their front yard, aglow from top to bottom with colorful lights and balls. Homer and I helped string the lights and were amply rewarded with holiday goodies.

Aunt Julie lived in a little house next door to Luke and Belle. Everybody called her 'aunt' even though she wasn't related to any of us. She appeared to be Native American, but nobody knew for certain. She loved flowers, gardening, and sitting on her front porch in the summer. One day, an old man appeared on the porch beside her, and he became Uncle Bill.

We speculated about who he was, and where he came from, but Aunt Julie wasn't talking. When I rode by on my bike, Uncle Bill would shout at me, "Hey, Red Fellow!"

The Grill was just past Aunt Julie's house, and was one of my favorite places. The owner was a grumpy man who would yell "What do you want?" whenever I walked in. It offered curb service, and sold hot dogs, milk shakes, hamburgers, and French fries. Inside was a long, L-shaped counter with stools. Under the counter, behind glass, was a mouth-watering display of candy bars, gum, and penny candies. There were booths, tables, and pinball machines. I miss the atmosphere of those old drive-ins. The Grill eventually became a residence, then a bar. In the 1980's, my mother purchased the building and transformed it into an antique shop. Now it belongs to me. It's across the road from my home, and housed my psychological counseling practice until my retirement. It awaits its next incarnation.

The Snake Man... Scotty lived up the road, near my Aunt Ruth. He caught rattlesnakes in the mountains, and displayed the rattling demons in cages in his yard. Tourists would stop, and Scotty would tell stories of his snake hunts. The more whiskey he drank, the better the stories. His hands and arms were scarred from encounters with the snakes. At Aunt Ruth's urging, Scotty donated a portion of his property and a church was built on the land. It still stands, bearing his name. It was my childhood church, and the home of my Vacation Bible School. I often wondered if Aunt Ruth coerced him into donating the land by suggesting that generosity might give him absolution for his drunkenness.

***

Gordon Freewill Baptist Church...had its own cast of characters. Pearle was the uncontested choir leader. She occupied the front row, corner seat, and belted hymns in a "joyful noise" that startled children and dogs alike. Stretch was a gentle giant who towered over everybody in the back row. He couldn't straighten up from working in low coal all his life, so leaned precariously over the row in front. As kids, we used to make bets on whether he would tip over completely, crushing the front row. In the summer, missionaries would come to teach bible school, and share stories about their travels to countries we read about in our geography books.

Money, Money...Charmco had one well-to-do family. The Crightons lived in the showplace of the community, not far from the church, with a paved driveway, rock walls, and patios. Mr. Crichton had been a mine owner, and a store manager. Dad would fill large baskets with vegetables from his garden, and I was drafted to deliver them to the back door of the mansion. It was intimidating to go there, but Mrs. Crichton was pleasant, with a musical southern accent, and paid me twice the asking price.

Fun And Games...My best childhood friend was a wiry little guy with a buzzed hair-cut, and a sweater always tied around his waist. My Dad called him Huck because he went along on my adventures. We built a clubhouse behind my house, and explored the wooded trails with the neighborhood kids. We had another friend, Kenny, who came from a family of ten kids. They lived near us in a five-room house similar to ours. We wondered where they all slept in that small house. He had a paper route, and got up at daybreak every day to deliver papers on his bike.

One night, when we were young teens, Kenny joined us on a camp-out near the river. He decided it would be fun to wake us the morning after the camp-out by dropping the tent on us. We had confiscated some of my Dad's grape wine the night before, so he was still feeling frisky. Instead of just untying the ropes, he decided to chop down the tree holding the ropes. We heard chop, chop, chop but thought Kenny was cutting firewood for a morning campfire. Suddenly, the tent dropped, and we heard Kenny shouting triumphantly as he rode away on his bicycle.

Days later, when the gang was gathered at my house, my Dad said, "You know that wine I made and put in the cellar? I gave some to friends of mine in Ohio and it killed one of them, outright." Everybody's eyes got big but nobody said anything. I recognized his tale telling. I had been educated at the master's knee. But my friends weren't as savvy. Dad had done it again.

The Crazy Ones...My Dad's friends all had their quirks. Walter always wore suspenders with Khaki shirts and pants. He had several gold teeth, and was known for his lies and exaggerations. He was also very gullible. Dad would send him on wild goose chases to fishing holes or hunting spots that didn't exist. Walter would return with incredible stories about those non-existent places.

Jim was a mine boss—a big, tough looking guy who drank all the time. He had a horse that would put its head through the kitchen window and eat and drink from the sink. Chickens and ducks roosted on chair arms inside the house. Jim's every sentence ended with "Huh." One day, his shotgun accidently went off in his brand new jeep. It blew out the dash, radio, everything. He responded, "I messed it up, huh." He drove the jeep that way for years.

E. P., The Peddler... Each day, E. P. would bring his horse, Maude, to graze in our field. He would then back his black and green Model T truck out of his garage, and head off down the road, truck over-flowing with pots, pans, dishes, spices, and tonics. His name was painted in big letters on each side of the truck. He wore the same bibbed overalls until they were so dirty, they could stand up on their own. Then he would buy a new pair. When he died, our next door neighbors inherited his storage building. It was three stories high, piled full of stock for his route, and curiosities he'd picked up in his travels. There were also enough spare parts to keep his old Model T truck running for years. The fortunate neighbors moved into the building, lived there, and sold the merchandise. They made enough money to live comfortably the rest of their lives.

The Moss Man... Our next door neighbor, Bill, helped to support his family by buying moss from the loggers in the mountains, and re-selling it to nurseries and florists. It was a good example of the ingenious ways miners supplemented their income when there was no work, or when they became disabled, and could no longer dig coal. Bill would fill hundreds of burlap feed sacks with moss, and store them until a truck arrived from Indiana to pick them up. My teen friends and I earned a little spending money loading the truck. His son, Billy, helped me build elaborate wooden carts that we dragged up the mountain and rode down. They had steering wheels and crude hand-brakes that seldom worked, making the descent unpredictable and exciting. We sometimes wound up with bruises and scraped knees -- unimportant battle scars of our adventures.

My continuing fascination with cars began with those wooden carts. In winter, we would fly down that same hillside on our sleds, my mother leading the pack.

Gypsies... We lived along a well-traveled highway, and it wasn't unusual for carloads of gypsies (in their colorful clothing and billowing scarves) to descend on the homes closest to the road, asking for food. I don't know where they came from, and they never created any problems for us. But as soon as they were spotted, the phones started ringing up and down the road, neighbors warning neighbors. It was rumored they were slick thieves. But my Dad gave them garden vegetables and fruit, treated them respectfully, and they went on their way. He did, however, use them as a threat when we were children and misbehaved. He told us the gypsies would come at night and carry us away. Scary...and it worked, at least for a few days.

I once asked my Dad how he and his siblings came to own their properties, side by side, along the highway. He told me Charmco was once called Duggansville. It was part of a large parcel of land owned by a Mr. Duggan. Dad, his brothers, and sisters all purchased their lots at land auctions. My paternal grandmother, Angie Spinks Canfield, was attending one of those roadside auctions when a speeding car lost control and crashed into the crowd, killing her instantly. She was forty-four, with a thirteen-year-old daughter, Kay, still at home.

Her son, my Uncle Guy, was a passenger in the car that killed her. Both Guy and the driver had been drinking, but charges were never filed. My Uncle Guy eventually moved to California and seldom came back to visit.

By the time I was old enough to hear the story, he had been gone a long time. I can only imagine how deeply it must have affected him. Thirteen-year-

Angie Gladys Spinx Canfield

George Jenkins Canfield
Paternal Grandfather

old Kay took over the cooking and management of the household. Granddad Canfield never remarried, and eventually moved in with his daughter, Ruth, and son-in-law, Jack.

"It's a small world" note...my maternal grandfather, Alvin Kuhl, helped to build the house they all lived in, and that family home now belongs to my son, Joshua. Many of the homes owned by my Dad's siblings were passed down to their children, my cousins, and later, to grandchildren of those original owners. There's something about this Appalachian mountain area that holds many of us here, generation after generation.

In the summer of 2016, a disastrous "100 year" flood devastated the small towns of Rainelle, Charmco, and Rupert. Other parts of Greenbrier county, and large areas of Kanawha County, were also severely affected. The towns were under six feet of water, and several people died. Few residents had flood insurance, so much of the clean-up and recovery depended on neighbor helping neighbor. Despite severe financial difficulties, businesses and residents rolled up their sleeves, and are working together to rebuild their homes and restore their communities.

It gives me great joy and satisfaction to continue to live in Charmco, and to be able to share the stories of family and small town life that are still so vivid in my mind. I plan to continue to pass them down to my children and grandchildren, in living color.

- Carl Edward Canfield

Aunts, Uncles And Cousins

Growing up in close proximity to aunts, uncles and cousins had its advantages. My Dad had two sisters, Kay and Ruth, and four brothers. The two sisters, and two of the brothers, Virgil and Earl, lived nearby. The other two brothers, Claude and Guy, moved across the country, to California, in search of better jobs, and maybe some privacy.

Among Dad and his siblings, there were sixteen first cousins, and numerous second cousins. All the houses faced a busy two-lane highway, State Route 60. When we were children, it was easy to avoid the highway as there were narrow trails cleared through the woods. The trails were behind all the houses, so it was easy to get from one house to another to play, or to hang out, as we became teenagers. It was an Appalachian style Kennedy Compound, without the money and swimming pools. With all those cousins, it was easy to find a playmate. And because there were so many of us, there were lots of birthday parties, camping trips together in the summer when the coal mines took its two-week hiatus, and vacation bible school, which we were all forced to attend.

Aunt Ruth was the self-proclaimed moralist of the family, backed up by her husband, Uncle Jack. In warm weather, he would pile all of the cousins into the back of his pick-up truck, and haul us to Sunday School, whether or not our parents chose to attend. Usually, none of the adults did. Aunt Ruth, almost single-handedly, managed to get a new church started and built, across the road from her house. Then we were all doomed to hellfire and brimstone sermons every Sunday because the church was close enough for all of us to walk, so there was no excuse. I was a teenager before I realized how strange it was for all those parents to SEND their children to church but seldom go themselves, except, maybe on Easter or for the Christmas pageant, to see us as angels, shepherds, or wise men.

The aunts and my Mom spent a lot of time together. None of the women drove, and it wouldn't have mattered if they did. If there was a family vehicle (usually a truck) the men claimed it. My Dad walked several miles, an hour each way, to work in the coal mines until he could afford a car. Everybody had big gardens, so the women would sometimes can vegetables or make preserves together. In winter, they would set up quilting frames and take turns completing each other's quilts. When I was little and hadn't started school yet, I would fall asleep at nap time, listening to the comforting hum of their voices.

The uncles all hunted and fished with my Dad in spring and summer. Deer season culminated in a week-long hunting/camping trip every fall. I'm sure the idea of getting away from their wives for a week was the most attractive feature of the outing. The moonshine they took along was a close second.

Most of the men in the family drank, a lot—cheap wine, home brew, and whiskey. My Mom didn't allow Dad to have his booze in the house, so he hid it in his ramshackle garage. I never understood what difference it made where he drank it. He couldn't disguise the fact that he was drunk. I guess it was Mom's way of pretending she was maintaining some control over an uncontrollable situation. When the old garage was demolished, we discovered hundreds of empty bottles. Unfortunately, the alcoholism (a word nobody in the family ever used) was passed on the next generation (my generation), resulting in jail terms, traffic deaths, and sad lives for many of my cousins.

There were some disadvantages to all that family togetherness. Everybody knew everything about everybody else. Scandals were passed around and discussed, but kept within the family as much as possible. When one of my cousins became pregnant, she was quickly sent away to stay with relatives until the baby was born. Then the parents took a trip, brought the guilty teen home, and announced they had adopted a baby. Everyone in the family, and probably the community, knew the truth, but kept up the facade. The rest of us were lectured loud and long on the evils and disgrace of having a baby out of wedlock. Pity the unlucky cousin who had to live with that stigma for years.

Childhoods were very different for us, growing up in the 40's and 50's. We were outdoors all the time in the summer, riding bikes, playing softball, marbles, jacks, or cowboys and Indians. At the time, we didn't realize we were one fourth Native American with a Cherokee great-grandmother, so the cowboys and cowgirls were always the good guys and the Indians, the bad guys. If I had known about our ancestry, I would have chosen the Indian role, and bravely defeated my brothers—those annoying cowboys.

Dress-up was a favorite game of the girl cousins. We turned an old storage shed into a playhouse, spending hours dressing up in our mothers old clothes, shoes, hats and having tea parties with our dolls. I also liked to play school. As the oldest, I was the teacher, and my younger siblings, Carl and Homer, were the students. I've been told I liked to make mud pies and,

28

on occasion, would feed them to those unsuspecting siblings. I have absolutely NO recollection of that and if they were willing to eat them...Reading was my favorite thing, but every time my mother caught me inside with a book, she would take it away and send me outside, with warnings of "ruining your eyes" with all that reading. We didn't have a television until I was in my early teens. Aunt Kay and Uncle Fred acquired the first TV in the family—a huge, impressive, wood console. We would all gather at their house on Sunday evenings to watch fuzzy, black and white variety shows.

As we became teenagers, my friends and I discovered a new pastime— gossiping on the phone. Even better was eavesdropping on the other people on the party line. It was great, until our parents caught us.

In summer, out-of-town relatives came for overnight visits. Most were happily anticipated. Mom would clean and cook for days. But one visiting group was always dreaded. This nameless aunt was terrified of germs. She always brought her own sheets and cooking pots, and insisted on preparing her family's meals herself, while her red-faced husband tiptoed behind her back and quietly apologized for her behavior. Again, that southern hospitality dictated welcoming smiles all around, but there were loud cheers as their car backed out of the driveway.

My favorite out of town visitors, besides my Grandma Bessie and Grandaddy Alvin, were Grandma's brother, Dorsey and his wife, Olive. They were easy-going and funny—the family gypsies, moving often, taking whatever jobs they could find, always enjoying life, and passing that joy on. Some family members frowned on their colorful, haphazard lifestyle, but I adored them, deciding later (in my adult wisdom) that they were just ahead of their time. They were hippies, before it was fashionable.

The Mickey Mouse Watch

On February 17, 1951, Daddy roused my six-year-old brother, Homer, and me from a sound sleep. He told us to get dressed, and we were going Aunt Ruth's to stay for a while. It was three days away from my eighth birthday.

I didn't know if a while meant tomorrow or forever. When I tried to ask about my mother, he looked worried and said she was sick, and Aunt Ruth would take care of us until she was better. That was it. No further explanation. He hustled us into our boots, coats and hats, rushed us past Mom's closed bedroom door, and into the cold, dark night. It was sleeting, and the icy pellets burned my cheeks and lips. Daddy started the car, and slid down the icy hill, pausing at the edge of the two-lane road. Homer and I held on tight as Daddy gunned the car to get out of the snowy, rutted driveway.

Aunt Ruth was waiting for us at the door in her old, blue robe, a worried look on her face. Daddy didn't even say goodbye; he just ran back to the car and headed down the road. The fire was crackling in the iron cook stove, and the sweet smell of chocolate warmed the room.

Aunt Ruth hugged us, helped us out of our heavy coats and put steaming mugs of hot chocolate into our freezing hands. Daddy had forgotten about our gloves in his haste to get us out of the house. I sat very straight and grown-up by her side, and waited. I was afraid to ask about my Mom.

About that time, Uncle Jack came into the room with a load of firewood, and his wide grin made me feel better. Things couldn't be so bad if Uncle Jack was smiling. He pulled the rocker over close to us, and explained that we were all going to drink our hot chocolate and go to bed. He said when we woke up in the morning, we would have a new baby brother or sister. Reading my worried eyes, he told me my Mom was going to be fine and I was not to worry. I believed him. Uncle Jack taught our Sunday School class. He would not lie. Aunt Ruth and Uncle Jack led us into the spare room, and we tumbled into the big feather bed. I was instantly asleep.

Daddy's voice woke me in the morning. Sun was shining through the frosty window panes, and I could smell bacon. "Get up, sleepy heads! You have a baby brother." I was disappointed the baby wasn't a girl, but what I really wanted to know was if my Mom was alright. Daddy explained she was sleeping, but he would come back after breakfast, and take us home. We gobbled Aunt Ruth's crunchy biscuits with strawberry jam, and washed them down with more hot chocolate. I could hear the rooster crowing in the hen house, and Sam, the coon hound, howling for breakfast. It began to seem like an ordinary day.

Daddy kept his promise, and took us home after breakfast. We tiptoed into the bedroom. Mom was propped up on pillows, looking tired but smiling and cradling a small bundle in her arms. "This is your new brother. His name is Carl."

Carl looked red and wrinkled, but I leaned over and kissed him anyway. Mom pulled two wrapped presents from under the covers. She handed one to Homer and one to me. He tore into his package and ran off, squealing about his new Hop-Along Cassidy gun and holster.

I opened the pretty paper carefully. When the package emerged, I couldn't believe my eyes. It was the Mickey Mouse watch I had wished for at Christmas— but didn't get.

"Happy early birthday, Sharon, " Mom said. I hugged her through happy tears. I didn't tell her I liked the watch better than the crying baby.

Epilogue: I still have the Mickey Mouse watch and, thankfully, my baby brother, Carl.

Letter To My Ten-Year-Old Self

Sharon June Canfield
1953

Congratulations to you and your best friend, Sandra, for winning second place in the county talent contest. The two of you have been singing duets since first grade; so of course you wanted to be in the contest, even though you were the youngest contestants. You worked hard, rehearsing after school with cousin Hazel on special choreography. You were so cute in your cowgirl outfits -- jeans, red plaid shirts and cowboy hats. Ricochet Romance was a great song choice. The harmony was perfect. I really don't think anyone noticed when you couldn't get the toy gun out of the holster for the grand finale. And I'm sure nobody could tell your heart was beating out of your chest; you were so nervous the whole time. Mom and Daddy didn't think the two of you were good enough be in the show. Maybe they were trying to protect you from disappointment. But you noticed they were grinning when you won. Mom didn't even scrub off the little bit of lipstick cousin Hazel had sneaked onto your lips just before you went on stage.

You were disappointed you didn't win first place. You got the loudest applause. It was hard for you to understand why the pretty majorette won, even though she kept dropping her baton and bending over to pick it up. Eventually, you'll figure all that out, and it will kick off a life-long women's lib campaign. You will become a strong, successful woman, and you will choose a profession that allows you to help other women be successful too. Sandra will be your forever friend. Don't worry; for you, the music never ends. Someday, you will sing with a remarkable, award-winning barbershop chorus, and this time there will be a first place win.

I wish I could say to you at 10, "Be brave. Stand up for yourself. Most of all, be patient. You will be loved and life will be good."

An Old Straw Hat And Leather Gloves

Over his lifetime, spanning 91 years, my Grandad wore many hats. Of German descent, he was born Homer Alvin Kuhl on February 23, 1894, in Gilmer County, West Virginia. This was a time when farms and houses were miles apart, and families were somewhat isolated. Some people had horses, mules, or buggies; walking was the primary mode of transportation. Logging and mining were the main occupations.

After doing both of those things in his early years, Grandad became the craftsman and carpenter I knew in my childhood and young adulthood. He gained experience early, building houses and small businesses in the nearby town of Rainelle. He and Grandma Bessie moved to Greenbrier County early in their marriage, and operated a small restaurant in Charmco, the town where my sister and I were born. Building materials were expensive and hard to obtain, so he constructed a

Carl Canfield

wood-framed tent, with a wooden floor, and that was their temporary home. It had a stove pipe rising out of the top of the tent to vent the cooking and heating stove. A young man with ambition, Grandad soon realized that earning a living in Charmco was not going to be possible. He made the decision to broaden their horizons. He became a master saw-filer.

Until he retired, Grandad traveled with companies that constructed power plants. He worked in West Virginia, along the Kanawha and Ohio Rivers, traveling also to jobs in Ohio and Indiana. Power tools were rare. Towering forms were built from wood to hold the poured concrete that rose hundreds of feet in the air, and served as smokestacks for the coal burning power plants along those rivers. As years went by, he was affectionately called Pop Kuhl by his younger co-workers. With hand vises and ten-inch, three-cornered hand-held files, he kept the handsaws and circular saw-blades sharp and glistening for the workmen who constructed the power plants.

The skills acquired at work came home with him. He became a competent framing and finish carpenter, and, ultimately, a furniture builder. Years after his passing, evidence of his talent can be seen in the homes of his grandchildren and great-grandchildren. He was generous with his beautiful furniture and intricately carved shelves, gifting them to friends and relatives.

Among my memories of Grandad Kuhl, one looms large and vivid. I was six or seven, visiting with my family at my grand-parent's home in Point Pleasant, West Virginia. I decided to gather and crack some black walnuts. There were trees bordering the property that yielded this rare and delicious treat. Easily locating a hammer in Grandad's workshop, I chose his prized table-saw as a resting place for the nuts. I knew a blow from the hammer would crush the heavy black shell so I could easily pick out the kernels and eat them. I didn't know the metal to metal sound would trigger the wrath of my Grandad, and send him flying into the workshop. With a rage I had never experienced from him, he hauled me by the scruff of my neck, up the stairs to the living room, and presented me to my grandmother with instructions to "Keep this boy out of my shop!"

She responded with an equal amount of rage. "Old Man Kuhl, don't you ever scare this child again!" He didn't.

I gained a new respect for my Grandad's tools that morning, which continues today, in my sixty-fifth year, as I work with that very same table saw, and his other well-worn tools, in my own workshop.

Generally, Mr. Kuhl, as my Dad called him, was a man of few words. Always with a wad of Copenhagen chewing tobacco in his lip, he would quietly go about the task at hand. It was a family trait. My Dad would often comment that a Kuhl Family Reunion consisted of a long, long drive to Gilmer County, a hearty, home-cooked picnic, and a few grunts exchanged with people we rarely saw, and often did not know. My Grandad always, always attended. After my Grandmother Bessie had passed and he could no longer drive himself, we still made sure he got there. The family knew this was a mainstay in his life. He never missed a reunion, until his death at ninety-one in 1985.

When I was 8 or 9 years old, my Grandad began a new tradition of a homecoming at his home in Point Peasant. This custom actually began at the home of Grandad's brother, Howard Kuhl. When Great Uncle Howard passed away, Grandad took over the homecoming. In late summer, assorted members of the extended family gathered at his home for a picnic of grand proportions. My family would arrive several days before the picnic to help with the elaborate set-up and preparation.

Grandad built picnic tables, which he connected with plywood bridges, to create a huge table stretching all the way across the front yard. The entire structure could be taken apart at the end of the day, and stored until the next year. The yard and shrubbery had to be meticulously trimmed and groomed. The flowers beds and rose garden were always in full bloom. The fruit trees, apple, peach, and pear, were full of summer's bounty.

The croquet court on top of the hill behind the house was like the finest golf course, covered with a special grass, and meticulously manicured. Wooden stakes, with holes drilled in the tops and painted white, were placed in the ground to accommodate the wire wickets.

Homer Alvin Kuhl and Carl Edward Canfield

The carefully measured court, the wooden mallets, and colorful balls all awaited the players, adults and kids alike. It was a favorite of all ages.

A huge pit was dug in the vegetable garden, and brush from that year's tree trimming was burned to provide hot coals for the corn roast. The coals were covered with sand, and the corn (in its husks) was placed on top of the sand. Pieces of old tin roofing were arranged on top to hold in the heat. The corn emerged lightly browned and juicy, ready for the hungry mob.

Vanilla and strawberry ice creams were hand-churned by reluctant grandchildren to top off the homemade cakes and pies that filled an entire picnic table. Just before the guests arrived, Grandad hung canvas tarpaulins over the tables, precisely positioned to protect from sun or rain. The show went on regardless of weather. No other family gatherings ever topped Grandad's homecomings.

My Grandad was very precise in everything he did. He could fix anything, and was always figuring out ways to make things work more efficiently. He moved slowly and deliberately through his day, and he didn't stop until his to-do list was completed. This pattern continued until just before his death. He thrived on having work to do, even at 90. In many ways, I became more and more like him as I matured, even adopting his habit of leaning on his garden hoe, leather-gloved hands grasping the handle, his head bent under his old straw hat, staring off into the distance, as if contemplating greater things than the daily chores. I think I know why he did that. I discovered it keeps people from asking a lot of questions while I'm sneaking in a short rest.

I have passed along Grandad's carpentry skills to my own son, Joshua. He now works in the construction field and has become more proficient than I ever was. He has new innovations in his toolbox, but also enjoys and is very good at precise finishing work.

Grandad's legacy continues, and it gives me great joy and satisfaction to know I played a part. I'm grateful he chose me to be his protégé, the keeper of his tools, and a part of the continuum of the family wood-working craft.

- Carl Edward Canfield

Grandma's Roses

The family legend is...Grandma Bessie Blaine Kuhl was mightily miffed when Grandaddy Alvin moved her out of town, and to the country. She was gregarious, loved shopping, and having lots of people around. Grandaddy was just the opposite. He hardly talked at all, and sought solitude. Apparently he won the argument, for off they went to the country, to build a house on a lonely dirt road.

Grandaddy must have known this decision would come back to haunt him. Grandma Bessie was a hot-tempered redhead. She came to love the home itself, but never let him forget that he had dragged her to this godforsaken place in the middle of nowhere. He was, however, a smart man, so he promised her a consolation gift of the best rose garden in all of Point Pleasant. And he delivered.

Every summer, in August, my parents, two brothers and I drove the five hours from our house to theirs to visit for a week. We left home when it was barely daylight so we could get there before the heat of mid-day. Those were the days before air conditioned vehicles, so the car got pretty miserable in the ninety-degree temperatures.

I adored my Grandma, who always smelled like apple pie and Evening in Paris, her favorite perfume. Grandaddy dutifully presented a bottle to her every Christmas. Grandma and I would spend early mornings in the rose garden. She taught me the roses had to be cut while the dew was still on the petals, to assure the sweetest fragrance. We chose the most perfect buds, arranged them in crystal vases, and placed them on crocheted doilies in the living room, dining room, bedrooms, and even the bath. She let me select the color for each room. On Sunday, we added daisies, and created multi-colored bouquets for the picnic table on the screened-in back porch. Grinning conspirators, we would sit there on Sunday and admire our handiwork while we devoured her delicious fried chicken, macaroni salad, baked beans, and lemon meringue pie. I still miss her, and think of that grin when I cut early morning roses in my own garden.

Every evening, I would see Grandaddy going out to the rose garden with his hose, watering the roses, and meticulously removing any weeds that had dared invade that sacred space. Once I heard him cursing under his breath at those damn roses. But he was careful never to let Grandma hear. He just weeded and watered and smiled.

I told you he was a smart man.

Chapter 2

Married With Children

High School Sweethearts

Sharon Canfield and Buddy Dorsey
Age 17 - 1960

Buddy Dorsey and I were sixteen when we met in History class. I had started first grade at age 5. Buddy had started at age 6 and been held back a year in elementary school. So I was a senior, and he was a sophomore. That alone should have doomed the romance. A senior girl just didn't date a sophomore boy, no matter how curly his hair or how irresistible his smile. But this girl decided to ignore the teasing of her friends about robbing the cradle, and go out with him anyway. Our first date was my very first date because my parents had decreed "no dating until you're sixteen." It was a Valentine sock hop in February, my Sweet Sixteen birthday month.

Unfortunately, it was West Virginia and February. On the day of the dance, it snowed all day, covering the roads, weighting down the trees. My Dad reversed his decision to let me go, delivering an emphatic, "No!" and walking out of the room. Mom backed him up, saying the roads were too slick. I knew it was useless to argue. They never listened to me when their minds were made up. I cried and cried but my tears were ignored. I couldn't call to cancel because Buddy's family didn't have a phone. So at 7 p.m., he knocked on my door, carrying a corsage of yellow roses, and looking like a dream in his navy blue sports coat. I looked at my Dad and waited. To my amazement, he went out into the storm, put chains on the car that Buddy had borrowed from his Dad, backed it out of the icy drive-way and sent us on our way, with a 10 p.m. curfew. I never knew for sure what caused the change of heart but Mom winked at me as we hurried out the door, afraid they would change their minds again.

Buddy kissed me goodnight at the door at 10 sharp. From that night on, we were an item. Against the wishes of both sets of parents, he asked me to go steady on prom night. Of course, I said yes. I graduated that year, and hated to think about leaving school and not seeing him every day. We were sure no one had ever been in love before—not like us. Between dates, we moped and dreamed, ignoring ordinary things like eating and sleeping. We watched the married couples around us, and wondered how they could sit for hours without saying a word to each other. There weren't enough hours in the day for us to say all the things we wanted to say. That summer after graduation was a golden one, filled with sunny, carefree days and romantic, moonlit evenings, despite the 10 p.m. curfew. We had no way of knowing our perfect world was about to crumble. My parents weren't blind. They could see wedding bells in our eyes and of course, thought we were too young, because we were only seventeen.

On a Thursday, in late August, out of the blue, they sat me down and announced that I was going to Sacramento, California. I would be living with my Dad's brother, Claude, and his wife, Dorothy, a school-teacher. I would be leaving on Saturday. Uncle Claude and Aunt Dorothy had been visiting the family in West Virginia and were starting the drive back on the week-end. I would be going with them and attending junior college there for a year.

I was told that I would need to take secretarial courses so I could get a job when I returned. They made it clear that I should not expect them to support me when I came back, for they would now need to focus on my younger brothers' education. My Dad truly believed educating girls was a waste of time and money. They went on to say that Buddy's parents agreed with the decision. When I came back...if we still felt the same...They didn't even bother to finish the sentences. They were sure our infatuation, as they termed it, wouldn't survive the separation.

None of my tears, pleadings or threats to run away prevailed. They knew I had no money, no driver's license and Buddy's dad had taken away his car privileges. He hitchhiked ten miles to see me before I left, and we both cried. On Saturday, my belongings were packed into Uncle Claude's long, sleek Cadillac. My younger brother was already moving into my room. Mom was tearful, but defiant, insisting again, this was the best thing for me. Dad was nowhere to be seen, dumping the burden of goodbyes on my Mom, hiding from the consequences of their shared decision. I wondered if he would miss me at all. It was a less than wonderful send-off.

California, Here I Come

I had tried for months to explain to my parents that I wanted to attend college after graduation and study journalism with a National Defense Student Loan I had earned with my outstanding academics. I had thought it through. Buddy had two more years of high school, and then planned to join the Army. We would get married when he finished basic training, and I could complete the last two years of school wherever he was stationed. When the NDS Loan offer came, my parents refused it without telling me. They feared I would drop out to marry Buddy, and they would be stuck paying it back.

They also didn't want me to attend a local college because, again, they were afraid I would elope or worse, get pregnant. They needn't have worried. Their loud and long speeches about the evils of pregnancy out of wedlock were burned into my brain. I suspect their fear of an elopement was based on their own history of having done that very thing when my mother was seventeen, and my father was twenty-seven. They were gambling on absence NOT making the heart grow fonder. In 1960 most of my friends did get married right out of high school. In retrospect, I guess their concerns were somewhat justified.

I went off to California, crying myself to sleep every night of the five-day drive across the country, and sending daily tear-stained letters to Buddy. Looking back, I'm surprised Uncle Claude and Aunt Dorothy didn't turn around, take me back home, and dump me on my parents' doorstep. They had no children of their own, and it must have been terrifying to have this sobbing teenager on their hands. I had no way of knowing, during that miserable trip, that the move would set the course for the rest of my life. It was the beginning of a grand adventure.

The farthest I had been from home was our annual family trip to visit my grandparents, who lived five hours away. I had never stayed in a hotel, or dined in a nice restaurant. My new home was in an exclusive gated community. It was an enormous brick rancher with a pool in the back yard. I had always known my Dad's youngest brother wasn't poor. Every two years, he and Aunt Dorothy bought a new Cadillac, and drove to West Virginia to visit with his siblings and their families, bringing gifts for all of us. I didn't realize how wealthy they were until I was unpacking my two small bags in my beautiful new bedroom, the first one I didn't have to share with a younger sibling.

I enrolled at American River Junior College the next day. Every day, Unc, as I nicknamed him, would drive me to school in the Cadillac, and pick me up after classes. The culture shock was huge but I discovered, to my surprise, that my southern drawl, which I didn't know I had, was an unexpected advantage. Boys, especially, thought it was charming.

I heeded my parents' warning about preparing for a job, and enrolled in business classes. The same small group of people kept turning up in all those classes, and we quickly became friends. They all came to swim in the pool in the back yard, carefully chaperoned by Unc or Aunt Dorothy. The leader of our little pack of eight was a year older and immediately became my mentor. Ray was engaged to a young socialite in San Francisco so we commiserated over our long-distance romances.

I was still writing undying love letters to Buddy every night. His letters, however, became less frequent and less loving. A friend finally told me the truth. He had hooked up with a girl in his class as soon as school started, and he was drinking a lot. When I confronted him, he admitted everything. He told me a year was too long to sit around and wait for me.

I expected tears and misery to descend upon me. Instead, I felt relieved. I was beginning to love my new life.

Ray went to San Francisco to spent Christmas with his fiancée and, like a character in a bad soap opera, also got dumped. Her wealthy parents had decided he wasn't good enough for her. To my surprise, he wasn't devastated either. Gradually, without either of us quite realizing how or when it happened, we were a couple—not just best friends. Our relationship had been effortless from the beginning. We had fun together. There was total trust. He was the intellectual equal that Buddy had never been. There wasn't the heart-pounding chemistry that had swept me off my feet that snowy night in February, 1960. But I liked this new, comfortable, adult-feeling relationship with Ray. Unc and Aunt

Ray Coker and Sharon Canfield
Sacramento, 1961
Unc and Aunt Dorthy's back yard

Dorothy approved. They trusted Ray, and allowed me to go on outings with him and our friends to L.A. and San Francisco, and ski week-ends to Squaw Valley and Lake Tahoe.

There were times, sitting around the table with Unc and Aunt Dorothy in their cozy kitchen, when I felt as if I had always lived there. As the months went by, I became comfortable with their successful friends. Unc told me stories of how he had worked himself up from a penniless soldier to a real estate mogul who owned half the Sacramento Valley. He talked to me like an adult, and he preached the importance of education, frugality, and sacrificing small wants for larger gains. He was proud of my triumphs at college, and reinforced my self-confidence in a way my parents had never done. They always seemed to expect the worst. He and Aunt Dorothy always expected the best. They planted seeds that would continue to inspire me to strive for the best in myself, and look for the best in others.

As the school year drew to a close, I dreaded going home. I felt estranged from my family and my life there, despite letters and an occasional phone call. I learned many years later, that Unc and Aunt Dorothy had contacted Mom and Dad early in my year there and proposed adopting me, officially making me their heir, since they were unable to have children of their own. My parents angrily refused and the idea caused a temporary rift between the two families. I wished I could stay in California. But Unc had decided to attend Palmer Chiropractic College in Iowa for three years and start a new career. Ray didn't want me to leave, but he did not make any commitments to me either.

On the last day of school, Unc and Aunt Dorothy threw a big going-away party for me. There was a fancy cake, presents, and Ray, constantly at my side.

When everybody went home, I packed and cried. I tried to tell myself that I had accomplished what I set out to do. I was an A student, and an accomplished secretary with marketable skills. I had made wonderful friends. At eighteen, I had gone places and done things I would not have thought possible a year ago. It was time to go home and be an adult.

Epilogue: When Uncle Claude and Aunt Dorothy passed away a few years ago--the last of that generation--they divided their fortune among the children of their siblings, leaving each of us, the nieces and nephews, a nest egg for retirement.

Back In The Hills

The trip back to Charmco was almost as sad as the trip to California had been. Coming home was a reality check. Everything looked different from my new perspective—smaller and shabbier. Buddy called as soon as he heard I was home. My cousin, Ginger, gave a little welcome home party for me. He was there, and so was the old spark between us.

I was torn because Ray was calling every night, begging me to come back, and get a job there. I took the path of least resistance, falling back into old patterns, spending time with Buddy and my high school friends. At the end of the summer, he asked me to marry him. I said, "yes," knowing an official engagement would have to wait a year, until he graduated. My parents were not happy, but were relieved at the year-long wait. Buddy's parents were ecstatic. I think they hoped I would save him from himself. His nightly drinking binges had stopped when I came home. He knew I wouldn't tolerate it. I had seen too much of that at home.

The day Buddy proposed, Ray called, as he had been doing all summer. He had gotten his scholarship to San Francisco State, had a job, an apartment and wanted me to marry him! If my answer was yes, he would send a plane ticket. He had been planning all this for months, but didn't want to tell me until everything was certain. He was that kind of person—practical and logical. I don't think it even occurred to him that I might go home and pick up again with Buddy. For selfish reasons, I hadn't told him. Strange as it sounds, I loved both of them.

Sadly, my return to my home environment had activated old insecurities. Buddy was a comfortable choice. Our parents liked each other. My two best girlfriends, who had married Buddy's two best friends, right out of high school, were pushing me toward that decision. We could all go back to hanging out together, like old times. My life would be predictable, like theirs. The chemistry was certainly there between Buddy and me. He was handsome—an Elvis look-alike, with sparkling green eyes, wayward curls falling down on his forehead, and a sexy mouth that begged to be kissed. We couldn't keep our hands off each other. I had those happily ever after stars in my eyes again.

Despite all that, I couldn't quite get Ray out of my mind. I tried to compare the two men, the two lives I was being offered. Loving Ray would be easy. We were best friends. He made me laugh. He was kind, dependable, and would

46

take care of me. I would be safe, secure. But a life with him meant uprooting myself again, moving across the country, and leaving behind everything I knew. The me I had become in California, was tempted by the possibility of a new, different kind of life. But without Unc and Aunt Dorothy there as a back-up plan, just in case it didn't work, the fears and insecurities won.

I wasn't brave enough to take that lesser known path. I tried to explain all that to Ray, crying into the phone. On the other end, he was crying too. He begged me to think about it, said he would be there if I changed my mind, offered to come out and meet my parents. I hung up the phone and cried all night because I had hurt him so badly. I never called him back.

I was afraid I wouldn't be able to refuse him twice.

City Girl

As the California chapter of my life closed, another was about to open. My Dad was a small town politician. He campaigned for local candidates, drove voters to the polls, and kept a sharp eye on happenings in the state capitol of Charleston, eighty miles away.

When he heard about a secretarial position in the governor's office, he announced that I was going to apply for it. I thought the whole idea was ridiculous. No governor was going to hire an eighteen-year-old with no job experience. I learned later, Unc had talked up my college successes and awards to my Dad. Now he was determined to take me to Charleston to apply for this important position. I knew my skills were good, but this was way out of my comfort zone.

On Thursday, August 2, 1961, against my better judgment, I walked determinedly into the reception room of the governor of West Virginia. As I stepped over the threshold, my tiny bit of confidence evaporated. Two glittering crystal chandeliers bathed the enormous room in a soft glow, blending the powder blue walls and lush azure carpet into one endless sea of blue. The room buzzed with the animated conversations of well-dressed men and women.

The activity seemed to generate from two desks at opposite ends of the rectangular space. Straightening my shoulders, I adjusted my pillbox hat and clutched my spotless white gloves. Randomly, I chose the desk on the right and willed my shaky legs to carry me across the room.

I had to stifle an impulse to flee. I was convinced every eye in the room followed me, questioning my presence there. Finally, I reached the desk and blurted out my mission. "My name is Sharon Canfield. I have an appointment with Mr. King, Executive Assistant to the Governor."

"Mr. King is expecting you, Miss Canfield," the tiny blonde receptionist answered with a warm smile. "Won't you have a seat?"

Thanking her, and sinking gratefully into the soft cushions of the nearest sofa, I relaxed and tried to sort out the scene. Blue and gold brocade sofas, and gold velvet winged chairs were grouped around the room. High backed chairs of mahogany and red velvet splashed bright spots of color here and there. Engrossed in my surroundings, I was startled to hear, "Miss Canfield, Mr. King will see you now."

"This is it," I thought, summoning all my courage, and entering the office at the right end of the room. A stocky, middle-aged man with thinning hair and dark-rimmed glasses asked me to sit down. He had a pleasant, deep voice. He began the interview. Despite the churning in my stomach, my voice answered his questions calmly. He explained that he would dictate a letter, and I would transcribe it on the typewriter. My clammy fingers had trouble holding the pen but I got through it. Mr. King then escorted me to the receptionist's desk in the big, beautiful room and asked me to transcribe my notes. My heart fell as I sat down at the unfamiliar electric typewriter and glanced around the noisy, milling room. Noticing my trembling fingers, the receptionist, who told me her name was Hildred, patted my shoulder and said reassuringly, "Just relax. Do your best and don't worry."

Heartened, I bent over the machine. A few minutes (and several crumpled sheets of paper later) I took the letter into Mr. King's office. He scrutinized the paper. When the suspense was becoming unbearable, a slow grin spread across his face. "Very good!" he said. "We test all our applicants this way. We have to be sure they can work well under pressure. You passed with flying colors."

I sank into the chair nearest his desk. "The job's yours if you want it," Mr. King went on. "Officially, you'll be my secretary, but you'll also work with the governor and the press secretary. Now, let's talk about salary."

Thank goodness I didn't say what I was thinking, Salary! I'd almost pay you!

My Dad did some scouting among his contacts in the city and found a room for me in the home of an elderly lady who lived within walking distance of the capitol building. My salary was $200 a month. My rent was $100 a month. I was rich. I lived on ham salad sandwiches and cherry cokes from the little drugstore next door to my rooming house. Occasionally, my landlady would take pity on me, and invite me to have dinner with her. Food was inconsequential. I was living in the big city and life was good.

Many of my high school friends were already working for the state government. It was the thing to do after high school—if you weren't getting married or couldn't afford to go to college. I could usually get a ride home with someone on the week-ends to see Buddy. I rode the city buses to go shopping. I didn't need a car. The only people my age who had them were my peers who had received a car as a graduation present. They were from well-to-do families.

A few months later, my cousin, Sandy, graduated from high school and got a job in Charleston too. We shared an apartment with two other friends from school. It was the upstairs of an old house. We had a living room/eat-in kitchen, two bedrooms and a bath. It was drafty and ugly, but we loved it. It was constantly filled with our friends and boyfriends.

The summer that Sandy graduated, we decided to take a trip to Daytona Beach in her new car. I don't recall what make or model it was, but it was small, red, with no air-conditioning and had a trunk the size of a hat box. We invited a couple of friends to go along to share the expenses. Our mothers sent us off with fear and misgivings and many *thou shalt nots.* Although we were all working and living on our own, we were only eighteen; mothers never stop worrying. I would understand that better when I was the Mom of a teenage girl.

We didn't care that it was a hot, miserable drive because we were so excited. We drove all night, singing *99 Bottles of Beer on the Wall* to stay awake. When we crossed the Florida state line, early the next morning, we tumbled out of the tiny car to pose for a picture.

Daytona Beach was alive with rock music, good-looking guys, and the scenery wasn't bad either. Sandy and I both had boyfriends at home, so we could only look. But the other two girls had a great time, working their way through all the *thou shalt nots.*

I LOVED MY JOB! I loved everything about it. I loved getting dressed in the morning in my business suit, my spike heels, my white gloves, and my hat. Yes, we wore hats and gloves to work every day. I loved walking to work and seeing the golden dome of the capitol building gleaming in the sunlight. I loved the clatter my heels made on the marble floors as I entered the building. I loved the Governor's beautiful reception room with its magnificent carvings and paintings; I loved my tiny office next door.

My colleagues were fascinating people. Hildred, who was the governor's personal secretary, became my mentor and my friend. We stayed in touch for years after I left my job there. The governor's press secretary/speech writer tutored me and allowed me to compose short public relations pieces for the newspaper.

The other two women on the Governor's staff were, like Hildred, much older than me. They all mothered me. Naomi was a psychic; she introduced me to a whole new world of unexplained phenomena. She told fortunes and could levitate objects. She delighted in raising tables and chairs off the floor as skeptics gawked in surprise.

Doris was a tall, striking blonde. She taught me more than I wanted to know about husband deception. She was a shopaholic with a husband who was determined to control her spending. So, she shopped on her lunch hour, bought gorgeous clothes, then changed before she left work, and wore the new things home. She insisted he never noticed the difference.

My boss, who insisted I call him Dick, (instead of Mr. King) was 36. He was witty and charming. He quickly decided I walked on water; of course, what all secretaries hope their bosses will think. In the 50's and 60's, secretaries took dictation, typed, filed, but they were also expected to serve coffee, shop for birthday presents, and occasionally baby-sit.

Sharon Canfield
1963
My office in the capitol building

Dick eventually fell in love, got engaged, and married. But when I first met him, he had no commitments, and was quite the Romeo. I was constantly bailing him out of jams because he would make two dates for lunch or forget the girls' names. It was never boring. I turned his escapades into fiction stories that were published in secretarial magazines – my first publications.

My boss appreciated all those times I covered for him, and repaid me by making sure I was invited to all the fancy events, and got to meet all the important people who came to see the governor. I was fortunate to meet Presidents John Kennedy, Harry Truman, and Dwight Eisenhower, who came to visit during the West Virginia Centennial Celebration. One of the most meaningful meetings he arranged was with Pearl S. Buck; I idolized her writing.

I was living in two very different worlds--the grown-up world of work and the week-end world of Buddy's senior year of high school. One day I was meeting a president, and the next I was shopping for a prom dress. I don't know why it worked, except for the simple fact that Buddy and I were madly, crazy about each other. He gave me an engagement ring on his graduation day; he sold his beloved hotrod to pay for it. A few days later, he was off to basic training with the Army. I went back to work and began planning a wedding. It would take place in six weeks when he returned from basic. Then we would ride off into the sunset to live happily ever after.

That was the plan.

Best Laid Plans

The six weeks of Buddy's basic training flew by. I missed him, but my time was occupied with bridal showers, luncheons, and shopping for a dress. There was also uncertainty about where he would be stationed, and if I could go with him. He had requested Florida or the West Coast. We both wanted to get away, and see some of the country. Dick was in mourning because I would be leaving, and he insisted on no resignation until we had orders.

We were married on August 20 (my parents 22nd wedding anniversary), 1962 in a small ceremony. Both families present and smiling, at last.

After a short, sweet honeymoon, Buddy left again for Indiana, and six more weeks of training. I went back to work, and we waited for those important orders, telling us where our new home would be. They came, but they weren't at all what we expected. Buddy was leaving in two weeks for Korea. He would be gone for a year. I was not allowed to accompany him. It felt to us like the end of the world. I remember hanging up the phone after he told me, and sitting in the darkness for the longest time, trying to assimilate the news. I was too stunned to cry. That night would be the worst of the three hundred sixty five+ to come.

My office family and my roommates closed in around me; hour by hour, the lonely days and months slipped by. We wrote letters every day—or at least I did. After a few months, Buddy's dropped off from every day, to two a week, to one a week, and then even less often. I worried a little, remembering the California year, but I kept reminding myself that we were married now.

He was just busy and written communication was never his strong suit.

I was grateful for the busy distraction of my job. I went back to keeping a journal because putting a problem down on paper had always helped me deal with it. I started a new tradition of writing a letter on my birthday, about the happenings of that year, both in the world and my life. I continued this practice for several years, sealing the letters in envelopes and saving them in a carved, wooden box. I didn't open them or re-read them for twenty-five years. When I did, it was a surprising window on the person I had been at nineteen, twenty, etc. It was also a historical look back at the world of the 60's.

***

February 20, 1962
Governor's Office, Charleston, West Virginia

"As I celebrate my nineteenth birthday, it is historically, the most important one of my life.

Astronaut John Glenn orbited the earth today and returned safely. I am in awe and filled with pride in the men and women who have worked so hard to achieve this near miracle. I can't help wondering, what's next? Where do we go from here? Where will we be, nineteen years from today? There are those who think we're tempting fate. Perhaps man wasn't meant to enter the heavens uninvited. But we have done it and from here on, there can be no stopping. Man's thirst for knowledge and the desire to conquer space will become more intense now and who am I to judge? Each of us must choose our own destiny.

Looking back on the past nineteen years, I am amazed at the giant steps civilization has taken. Looking ahead to the next nineteen, it is with confidence and again, a great sense of pride in our country. My own future seems unimportant and small compared with the tremendous event I have witnessed today. I only hope my generation will be big enough to step into the shoes of the heroes of the past. May we make our ancestors proud and may we leave to future generations a sound and secure America, within a peaceful world. What's next? Where do we go from here? Onward and upward. After today, the heavens are our playground."

***

February 20, 1963
Governor's Office, Charleston, West Virginia

"Well, here it is, 1963, West Virginia's 100th birthday. It doesn't seem possible that a year has passed since we put our first man in orbit and the

54

space race began. So much has happened in my own life in the past few months. Last year at this time, Buddy was still in high school, we were just dating and I was still a teenager. Twenty seems like such a silly age, kind of in-between, not completely adult but not a teenager anymore. I suppose that means I'll have to change a few things, act more grown-up, and all that jazz. Last year, I felt on the edge of momentous things and I was right—Buddy's graduation, our engagement, his enlistment in the Army, our wedding, and now this nothingness while he's in Korea for a year. I am trying to be optimistic and concentrate on the future. Who knows what next year will bring, only as much as we put into it, that's for certain. 1963, you came in pretty mildly but I'm sure you're going to go out with a bang. Time passes so quickly, in the blink of an eye. We must grasp it and hold it and put as much into it as we possibly can. Treat us kindly, 1963, for we're plunging in, head first."

***

November 22, 1963
Governor's Office, Charleston, West Virginia

"History repeated itself today. The President of the United States, John Fitzgerald Kennedy, was assassinated. Our state, the nation and the world is stunned and grief-stricken. We received the news in our office that the president had been shot with disbelief. Our press secretary got a call and ran out of the office. He returned, pale and trembling. The president has been shot!

Everyone in the office gathered around portable radios, united by fear and sorrow. We prayed for the life of the President, strengthened by the bond that joins people in times of distress. When the announcement came that he had died, we all wept. The prayers of the peoples of the world are with the Kennedy family tonight and we are humbled by the realization of the mortality of man."

Camelot Lost

The streets of my city are empty and silent today.
Helplessly limp flags hang at half-mast.
Heavy, gray clouds darken the golden dome
of the W. Va. capitol, where I work.

I cry alone on the cold, concrete steps
of that shuttered building,
remembering a young man with sparkling blue eyes,
and a warm, firmly reassuring handshake.

I recall the thrill of meeting him,
and my amazement that he would take time
from national crises,
to attend our states 100th birthday celebration.

I grieve for my mountain people
who invested so much hope in him.
I grieve for the promise of better days.
I grieve for the wife and young children he left behind.

I feel a sad kinship with the people of my town,
and all the others around the country and the world,
who huddle in front of televisions,
trying to accept the unacceptable.

Tomorrow, we'll all try to figure out how to move forward.
But yesterday, President John F. Kennedy was murdered.
Today, his extended family weeps angry, anguished tears.
November 23, 1963

Homecoming

On a cold, bright day in December, 1963, the call I'd been waiting for finally came. Buddy was in Chicago. In three short hours, we'd be together again. I was nervous. How would we look to each other after a year apart? Would that special enchantment still be there?

I barely recognized the good-looking soldier stepping off the plane. He was taller, heavier, and carried himself with an assurance he'd never had before. Even his smile was different—more subdued. I missed the sparkling excitement that filled his eyes when he saw me, after even the shortest time apart. I knew it would be all right when I was in his arms again. I ran to meet him; his embrace felt wooden, and his kiss was a perfunctory peck. On the drive to the apartment, we found ourselves with nothing to say. I'd known we would need to get re-acquainted, but I hadn't anticipated anything like this.

My roommates had vacated the apartment for the week-end. Before they left, they cooked us a special dinner and filled the bedroom with candles. I had dreamed of this quiet, candle-lit evening for thirteen lonely months. But Buddy had other ideas. The minute we were inside the apartment, he called several friends, and invited them over to celebrate his homecoming. Why was he avoiding being alone with me? The friends brought beer, and when they finally left, after midnight, Buddy was roaring drunk. He passed out on the couch. I crawled into my bed alone, terrified of the morning. I kept thinking, this is the California rejection all over again, except worse. Now he's my husband.

It was worse. When he woke up, hung-over and depressed, I took a deep breath and asked him if he still loved me. I expected him to take me in his arms and make it all right. Instead, he looked at me for a long moment and replied, sadly, "I don't think I do."

I collapsed on the couch, the breath knocked out of me. For the next hour, I sat there and listened while my husband told me about Kwan, the Korean girl he'd been living with for the past seven months. I felt as if I had died, and some other woman was inhabiting my body. I tried to nod calmly, and ask questions. Did he love her? He didn't know. Did he want a divorce? No. So what now? He didn't know. At that point, something cracked inside me, and I ran into the bathroom, crying so hard I threw up.

When there were no tears left and I could think again, so many things began to fall into place -- the forgotten birthday, the tardy anniversary card, the decreasing stream of letters that said less and less. I had rationalized it all away, and now I was as angry with myself as I was with him. When I emerged from the bathroom, he was gone. I was glad. I didn't want to give him the satisfaction of knowing how much he had hurt me. I needed to salvage my pride, at least.

It was pride that kept us from separating immediately. Neither of us wanted to listen to the family saying *I told you so*. We went home the next day, pretending to be happy, reunited newly-weds. Everybody bought it—even our best friends. There were times, during the happy reunions, when I could almost believe the pretense that we loved each other. But when we were alone, we were strangers. With Buddy's 30-day leave nearly up, I didn't know what to do. I could go back to my job. Dick hadn't replaced me yet. But I would have to face my friends' well-meaning sympathy. I couldn't live with my parents. The list of options was short.

When the orders arrived for Ft. Eustis, Virginia, we drove out to the park, and sat in the car. There was no more time for pretense. To my surprise, Buddy asked me to go with him. I didn't know how to feel—happy, relieved, terrified. He made it clear he wasn't making happily ever after promises but he didn't want to give up on us either. I was clear-headed enough to know I was probably setting myself up for more pain if I agreed. In the end, I made the decision to go with him because I still loved him, despite his infidelity.

I decided to take the risk.

Life Goes On...

February 20, 1964
Ft. Eustis, Virginia..

"So much has happened this year. Civil Rights issues have split our country and people. Never, since the Civil War, has this strife been so contentious. Our hearts were so filled with hatred, we assassinated our beloved President Kennedy. The bullet was released by a demented ex-communist, but he was a product of our times. Perhaps it is some comfort to the Kennedy family to see how his death briefly knit our country together with love and compassion. Why couldn't we maintain that?

Personally, this has been a year of great victories and great disappointments. My despair when Buddy left for Korea made me more aware and appreciative of the friends who stepped up to support me at that difficult time. I'm proud I held my head up, worked hard at my job and battled through the loneliness. After all that, I welcomed my husband home after thirteen months, only to learn he no longer loves me. I've gone from disbelief, to fury, to reluctant acceptance, to a tiny ray of hope that keeps me fighting for the love we had. We found a small trailer near the army base and I'm in the process of making it home. There are other military couples in the trailer park so we're making new friends. I have no idea what this year will bring or where I'll be on my next birthday."

***

February 20, 1965
Ft. Eustis, Virginia...

"Hard to believe another birthday has rolled around. I've always heard that time goes faster when you're happy. So different from 1963 when Buddy was gone and the beginning of 1964 when things were so wrong with us. I can't pin-point when things started getting better, but it was sometime after I went back to work. I got tired of sitting at home while Buddy was at work. One day, I rode the bus to the Employment Office, booked an interview for a secretarial job with a large plumbing company. They hired me on the spot and I am now Executive Secretary to the president of the company. It isn't easy. I have to leave at dawn and change buses twice to get there but the pay is good and my self-confidence is returning. When I became independent again, making new friends, creating a new life for myself, Buddy started to notice, became more attentive. It's been a little like falling in love, cautiously, the second time around. I don't trust it yet, but I'm hopeful.

The outside world continues to be a scary place and the Vietnam War goes on, casualties mounting. We live with the fear that Buddy might be sent there but I try not to dwell on it."

***

February 20, 1966
Williamsburg, Virginia...

"Our class reunion was in September. My friends seemed little changed--looking a little older, maybe a little wiser, but basically, the same kids I graduated with five years ago. It is hard to remember they are grown adults with children of their own. Perhaps because we have no kids, I feel younger, more free. Buddy's out of the Army at last. I'm thankful he escaped Vietnam but still wondering about this war. How far will it go? What will be the final outcome? Never worried about nuclear war before. Seemed impossible. But I worry about it now. Makes me feel that all of us spend too much time working and planning for the future and too little time enjoying today. I especially feel this way since we've moved to Williamsburg. I won that battle. Buddy wanted to move back to West Virginia and work in the coal mines like his Dad. I couldn't bear the thought of that kind of life. Fortunately, a friend offered him a job selling life insurance for Prudential. Unfortunately, he's gone all the time. I know it's necessary for his success. But I keep asking myself if success is all that matters. Seems to me, time together should matter too. So many questions. So many decisions. I found a job in Williamsburg, managing an optometrist's office. I'd like to go back to school but Buddy thinks that's a waste of time and money. Sounds alarmingly like words I heard from my father. It's that male mentality of women should stay at home and raise kids. I agree that's important too. But can't we do both? Hard to find a balance."

***

February 20, 1967
Williamsburg, Virginia...

"Twenty four! So much happened last year. We bought our very own house--a sweet, frame house with cheerful green shutters and a big back yard. We think it's beautiful. I doubt any other house we own in the future will ever be as special as this one. Buddy made it through his first year with

Prudential. He's still gone a lot. Sometimes I'm more lonely than I was when he was in Korea. When he's gone at night, I write. Sold a story to McCalls Magazine – amazing! They paid me $1000 – a fortune to us. Thought Buddy would be so excited for me. He wouldn't even take the time to read the story.

Wish I didn't feel so alone. But maybe that's what makes a good writer-- feeling alone and wanting to reach out to others. I'd like to do that with happy stories that show life is good and dreams do come true. Guess that's my happily ever after syndrome again. We need that in our world, especially now, with the war taking so many of our boys and no end in sight. I never quite shake the fear that Buddy will be called back. So many of our friends and relatives are living with that same fear."

***

February 20, 1968
Williamsburg, Virginia...

"Another year and a happy one for us, at least the latter part of the year. Buddy left Prudential to go to work for an investment corporation. The change wasn't a minute too soon. He's home most nights and we are beginning to live like normal people again. I think he may have found his niche with this job. He's charming, likes wining and dining clients. I do admit, I worry about the wining part of the job. But he's happy and I'm happy to have him home more. He wants to have a baby soon. I hope we're ready for the changes that will bring. It would mean postponing my dream of going back to school, but I'm twenty-five, we've been married five and a half years, and our parents are clamoring for a grandchild. I guess it's time. Exciting but a little scary. Family was a big focus this year. We lost Grandpa Canfield at eighty-nine, but it was comforting to know he had a long, full life. Grandma Bessie and Grandaddy Alvin celebrated their 50th wedding anniversary. I wrote a special poem and read it at their party.

The world situation is worrisome. The war is constantly in the news. We're lucky that none of our immediate family have been called to fight. Now there's a flare-up in Korea. My fingers are crossed until June, when we can hang Buddy's official discharge on the wall and breathe easier."

The Ballad Of Bessie And Alvin

Bessie Blaine Godfrey and
Homer Alvin Kuhl
on their wedding day - 1918

Once upon a time, 1918 was the year.
There lived a girl named Bessie,
and she really was a dear.

She was young and single,
till there came into her life,
a shy and handsome stranger,
and she soon became his wife.

Alvin loved his pretty Bessie.
That was plain for all to see,
and it wasn't long before
there was a baby on his knee.

Baby Charles soon had a sister,
red of hair and fair of face.
Macil June, they called their daughter,
dressed her in a gown of lace.

Then the years, they seemed to vanish,
much like summer into fall.
Toil and sadness, joy and laughter,
Bess and Alvin knew them all.

Baby Charles grew into manhood.
Tall and straight and strong, he grew.
And one day he married Cora.
Love had blossomed, love anew.

Baby June became a woman,
slender, lovely, full of life.
Carl pursued her, loved her, wooed her.
Laughing June became his wife.

Came the years of new-found freedom,
quiet walking, side by side.
Once again, came baby laughter,
Grandma's joy and Grandad's pride.

Three were boys, all rough and tumble,
leading Gramps a merry chase.
Two were girls to kiss and cuddle,
leaving dolls around the place.

Bessie and Alvin
50th Wedding Anniversary
1968

So the years have hurried, scurried.
Fifty rich, full years have flown,
since the shy young man named Alvin,
chose sweet Bessie for his own.

Now we gather, friends and loved ones,
both from near and far away,
to salute you, Bess and Alvin,
on this very special day.

May the past hold shining memories.
May the present please you, too.
In the future -- joy unending,
like our love for both of you.

February 20, 1969
Williamsburg, Virginia...
"We made that parenting decision. I got pregnant almost immediately, and our parents are ecstatic. It's been an easy pregnancy. We turned one of the bedrooms into a darling nursery; Buddy refinished a beautiful crib; we have the bassinet I slept in as a baby; and come June, our new baby will sleep there. I wrote this letter with a heart full of joy."

Letter To An Unborn Child

Today, for the first time, your dad and I felt you move. It was a thrill unlike anything I have ever known. Suddenly, you weren't just an unknown factor; an exciting date on a calendar. From the moment I felt those first faint movements, you became a real person to me—an individual reaching out for life. At the moment, it matters not to us whether you are a strong, mischievous son, or a dainty, beguiling daughter. We only pray you will be born with the precious gift of health, enabling you to grow and learn.

When you make your long-awaited entrance into our world, you will receive many elaborate birthday gifts from loving friends and family. My own gifts to you may seem ordinary by comparison, but I believe they are the most important things I could ever offer you.

I would like to give you the security of a happy home, with parents, brothers, and sisters who love and respect one another. Your growing-up world will be much different from mine, but I want you to experience the same wonder and discovery. Perhaps there won't be as many forests for you to explore or sparkling, unpolluted rivers to fish, but there will be trees to climb and sweet-smelling clover to lie in. And always, I hope, there will be dreams to dream.

Many things will be easier for you than they were for your parents and grandparents. Your education won't begin, as mine did, in a three-room school warmed by a pot-bellied stove, but in a modern structure of stone and glass. No doubt, your teacher will be well-educated and equipped to handle a roomful of boisterous first graders, but I hope she will also be as kind and genuinely concerned as the magnificent woman who ruled our school.

I'm grateful that you will be spared many of the hardships of earlier generations, but I hope you won't miss the exhilaration of successfully meeting and conquering difficulties. I would like you to learn at an early age, as I did, that the best things in life aren't always those most easily attained.

More than anything else, I want you to grow up happy and contented with yourself and your world. And if the world of the future doesn't please you, I hope you will have the courage and conviction to do your part to change it. These are high hopes and expectations for one as yet so small. But if we could, we would give you all these gifts of life and more, for you are so precious to us, fashioned from the fabric of our love and our dreams for the future.

Your Loving Mother

February 20, 1970
Williamsburg, Virginia....

"Steven arrived June 16, 1969, and was declared by parents and grandparents to be the most perfect baby ever born. There was a glitch -- he managed to execute a somersault while I was in labor, so my doctor had to perform a C-section. The second glitch came when we arrived home from the hospital. Steven didn't want to sleep. And we did. He won that battle. He slept when he wanted and I slept when I could. Mom stayed with us for three weeks and took the night shifts so I could rest from the surgery and Buddy could sleep and be able to work. I quickly learned that napping equals survival. It's a new, wonderfully crazy life. I wrote this poem between feeding, changing, and constant laundry."

Steven Forrest Dorsey
1971- Age 2

Little Boys

Little boys are full of fun.
We know that now that we have one.
He hooked us with that toothless grin.
We'll never be the same again.

He'll trash the house with trucks and cars.
He'll pound his drum till we see stars.
He'll toddle all around the place.
We'll have a hard time keeping pace.

Some days we'll wish we had a clone,
so we could sit when we come home.
We'll worry like all parents do,
and think, sometimes, we've not a clue.

But children care not what we know.
What matters is the love we show.
And when we put them down to sleep,
we vow each night that love to keep.

That little face we kiss goodnight,
has now become our favorite sight.
We've months and years of fun to come.
We'll treasure all, even the drum.

Our Pioneer Christmas

I grew up in a family of Christmas Crazies, led by my mother, who always over-indulged in decorating, present-giving, and cooking massive amounts of food. One of my favorite Christmases was an old-fashioned one spent in a tiny hunting cabin, deep in the Appalachian Mountains. Mom, Dad, and my teen-aged brother, Carl, went up early to cut wood for the heating and cooking stoves, and hunt for the turkey. My oldest brother, Homer, convinced his city bride, Ann, to go. He told her a little white lie—that there were no bears in the woods. Buddy and I worried about the combination of no electricity or running water, and how we would care for our six-month-old son, Steven. But Grandma Bessie and Grandaddy Alvin were coming, and they wanted to meet their first great-grandson. So, armed with warm clothes, diapers, and high hopes, we left our home in Williamsburg and headed for the hills.

A narrow, cow-path road took us off the interstate and about ten miles into the wilderness. I glanced back at Homer's car as we bumped along and splashed through rocky creeks. Ann looked stunned. I wondered if anyone had dared to tell her the bathroom was a drafty, wooden shed about ten yards from the cabin. When we arrived, the windows were aglow with twinkling lanterns, and the frosty night was fragrant with spicy pumpkin and mincemeat. Mom was bending over the huge, wood-burning monster that turned out delicious, though occasionally untimely, meals. Her cheeks were pink, and her eyes sparkled with the excitement of the whole family being together for Christmas. We hugged all around and fought for space near the stove.

Early the next morning, the men, led by Dad, marched off to find the perfect tree. Ann and I strung popcorn and made construction paper decorations while Mom cooked. Steven played nearby, and Grandma dozed in the rocker by the stove. As she was buttering the turkey, Mom confessed that she, not Dad, had shot the bird when she was outside getting water from the spring. We giggled as she described Dad's shocked expression when she came in carrying dinner.

The men came home with a perfectly-shaped pine that would barely go through the door. We draped it with our popcorn strings and paper creations, and declared it beautiful. Mom outdid herself with a delicious turkey dinner with all the trimmings, followed by four kinds of pie, including Grandma's renowned lemon meringue. We had all agreed to keep presents at a minimum because of the limited space, but piles of gifts appeared from behind chairs and hidden corners. Paper and bows flew, amidst much overstuffed groaning and laughter as Steven tried to eat the trims.

At dusk, Granddaddy carefully lit the candles and lanterns around the room. It was as if dozens of tiny fireflies had come to rest in the cabin. Steven crowed and waved his chubby hands, content on Grandma's lap. As I looked from one much-loved face to the other, it seemed a circle of life was complete. I didn't know it then, but it would be Grandma's last Christmas. I just knew it was a Christmas like no other that I would always remember.

Stay At Home Mom

I loved being a stay-at-home Mom. I had friends in the neighborhood. I became a master crafter, and filled the house with my creations. I joined *Sweet Adelines*, a women's barbershop chorus, which gave me a couple nights out of the house each week and a chance to sing again. I made wonderful friends who are still my best friends today. Buddy encouraged my involvement in *Adelines*. He liked having daddy time with Steven. Both sets of parents came to visit often, and we went to West Virginia to spend most holidays. Three years flew happily by, and sometimes I had to pinch myself to believe it.

In 1973, Buddy decided to change jobs, becoming a mortgage banker. He was very successful and making more money, so we decided to find a piece of land, and build our dream house. We found the perfect acre, cleared the lot ourselves, and did a lot of the finishing work on the house. We splurged on new furniture, finally getting rid of our hand-me-downs and thrift store stuff. The finished product was gorgeous. Everything should have been wonderful, but Buddy was not satisfied. He started talking, again, about moving back to the mountains, and living close to his parents. We fought about it a lot. I didn't object to living near his family. I objected to the whole idea of moving back to the area. There were no jobs, the schools were sub-standard, and I knew there was no future for us there. For once, my parents agreed with me. I liked living in Williamsburg, loved our little family, our new home, and our many close friends.

About the time the fights over moving were fiercest, I discovered I was pregnant. Steven was almost old enough for kindergarten. The pregnancy was a little unnerving. I knew I would face another c-section. Buddy's state of mind was also unsettling. But to my surprise, he was so excited at the news, he agreed to back off the moving dialogue. We both hoped for a little sister for Steven.

This pregnancy was the exact opposite of the first one. I was sick and on the couch for most of the nine months. But I forgot all of that when I saw our black-haired daughter, looking like one of the famous Beatles, with a mop of thick hair, and wide eyes that already looked wise. It was love at first sight. We took Shannon home to our wonderful new house, an adoring big brother, and two sets of grandparents who had arrived with every pink, frilly thing they could find. I settled in, again hoping for that happily ever after.

71

My Mommy

Shannon was a never-ending source of fun- -good-natured, trailing after her big brother as fast as her chubby, little legs would carry her; loving all over us and everybody who came to visit. If she could have written poetry at that young age, I think it would have sounded something like this.

Shannon Blaine Dorsey
1976-Age 2

My Mommy makes cookies and sings songs to me.
She stops what she's doing to sit down for tea.

When dolly fell down and busted her head,
she wrapped her in blankets and put her to bed.

I help in the kitchen and Mommy just smiles,
when I take all the pots and make falling-down piles.

My fun time is morning, when Mommy gets dressed
and puts on her lipstick and all of the rest.

She dusts me with powder and paints my nails pink.
Then I get some lip gloss and perfume that stinks.

We march out to breakfast and Daddy smiles too,
and cooks lots of pancakes with strawberry goo.

A House Of Cards
1976

Sadly, ever after was short-lived. Buddy came home one day and announced that he had been offered a transfer to Roanoke, Virginia, and had accepted. We were selling the house, and moving immediately. Some digging revealed he had asked for the transfer because it would put him within two hours of our hometown, and he had taken a big pay cut to get the job. I was dumb-founded. I didn't want to leave all the things and people I loved. He didn't care. He said, "I'm going, with you or without you. Stay here, if you want." I was too shocked by his nasty, hateful tone to respond. How could this be happening again? I did think about staying in Williamsburg, but I hadn't worked in years, didn't have a car or money of my own. Steven was in school; Shannon was barely two, and would have to go to day care. Excuses of a frightened woman? Yes. There were no good choices. And again, I took the path of least resistance.

A few days later, our dream house went on the market. My friends and I cried through going away parties. My Sweet Adeline chorus sang goodbye songs to me. Devastated, I packed and moved to Blue Ridge, a small community outside of Roanoke. Buddy had gone earlier to find a house and start his new job. The job turned out to be my worst nightmare. He traveled a lot, socialized with his co-workers at night and was drinking heavily again. I felt betrayed, abandoned and traumatized. Had I known he was beginning to dabble in drugs, I would have been terrified.

That still, small voice inside my head told me I needed to get a job, just in case...but every time I brought it up, it triggered a new fight. My job, he kept reminding me, was taking care of the house and our children. So I compulsively polished and shined the new house, resumed crafting on a grand scale, filled journals with my discontent, and hoped it would get better.

For months, we lived with an uneasy truce. Buddy became more irritable, and distracted. He bought a motorcycle, started dressing differently, and wearing strands of gold chains. I thought—it's just mid-life crisis; he'll get over it. Then he stopped coming home for dinner; sometimes, he didn't come home at all. When he did wander home in the wee hours, he was disoriented, and reeked of alcohol. I tolerated it, made excuses for him, and lived in denial.

The end came just before Christmas. He told me he was moving out of the house into an apartment with his new girlfriend; he wanted a quick divorce. He went on to say he wanted to be free to drink and party; he didn't want to be tied down to a wife and children. It was clear there would be no negotiating. I now wanted out as much as he did. I began to formulate a survival plan for the three of us.

I did get revenge. When he went to work the next morning, I beat his new golf clubs to death over his new motorcycle.

The incident was never mentioned by either of us.

When Loving Isn't Enough

When being together brings us more pain
than joy,
my loving you isn't enough.

When we talk and there is no resolution,
loving you isn't enough.

When I want more than you're able to give,
loving isn't enough.

When you confess to loving someone else,
I have to face the truth.
My loving you was never enough.

Endings...

My swallowed tears,
hidden pain.

Your echoing footsteps,
a closing door.

Silence.

Chapter 3

Single Parenting

Survival Plan

We spent the month of December working out the legalities of the separation. Buddy agreed to everything I asked. He was making good money, and was willing to pay extra support until I could get a job. We decided to postpone telling the kids and our families until after Christmas. We happy-faced our way through the holidays, but looking back at the photos, there wasn't much happy.

When I told my family, they immediately lined up on Buddy's side, assuming I had done something to cause this disaster. As I said earlier, he was charming. I wasn't surprised by my brothers' reaction. Buddy was their friend. Guys stick together. My mother's placement of blame hurt more. We told Buddy's parents together. He admitted the affair and assured them, to my surprise, that none of it was my fault. He took complete responsibility. However, as they left our house that night, Buddy's Dad said to me in a low voice, "This is all your fault. If you had been a good wife, this wouldn't have happened." That set the tone for all future communication. They wiped me out of their lives, and gradually, over time, their grandchildren also. It was as if we never existed. The message was clear—our son can do no wrong.

Telling Steven and Shannon was one of the hardest things I've ever had to do in my life.

All four of us cried. Buddy left that night, and I can still see nine-year-old Steven pounding on his upstairs window and screaming, "Daddy, please don't go!" as he backed out of the driveway. Shannon was four, and confused by the drama but she absorbed more than I thought. Years later, she told me how scared she was. She became very protective of me, staying close, hugging me, patting my arm. That night would haunt each of us in a different way, for a very long time.

Faced with the lack of emotional support from either family, I began to formulate a survival plan. I didn't want to remove Steven from his private school mid-year. Shannon was already attending a Montessori School two days a week. We upped that to five, and I took a temporary job there so I could be nearby during this adjustment period. When the temp job ended, I found a full-time position writing copy for a public relations firm. Buddy drove Steven to school so he was able to see his Dad every day, which seemed to ease his anxiety.

The long range plan was to move back to Williamsburg where I had friends, and a support system. I put the house on the market, hoping it would sell by the time school was out for the summer. My days fell into a pattern—take Shannon to Montessori, meet Buddy there with Steven, go to work, reverse the routine in the evening, make dinner, do homework, put kids to bed, and cry. I called my friends in Williamsburg daily. Their love and support was my stability. I filled journals with my fears, my anger, my loneliness, and concerns that my children were going to be scarred by this divorce. I had absorbed the guilt heaped on by both families. It was a crushing burden. I wrote this poem during that time. It was published in a single parent magazine, boosting my shattered self-confidence and encouraging me to continue writing.

Prayers Of A Single Mother

Help me sit through the Star Wars Trilogy
one more time with my nine year old son,
without becoming paranoid.

Slip me some reassuring answers at bedtime,
when my little girl, smelling of bubble bath
and bubble gum, asks, "Is Daddy coming home?"

Give me a sense of humor for those days
when the car won't start,
and the vacuum cleaner revolts.

Give me enough mechanical know-how
to recognize that I only need a tune-up,
not a new transmission, as the garage claimed.

Teach me, quickly, how to whittle a miniature car
from a block of wood,
in time for next week's Pinewood Derby.

Teach me to see the positive in my new chores.
Help me to enjoy house painting and grass mowing,
when I'd rather be baking cookies.

Transform me into a financial genius,
who can stretch four weeks pay,
through five long weeks.

Give me a reserve of energy
at the end of my working day,
to begin my other working day at home.

Endow me with forgiveness
for the husband and father who deserted us.
Replace the anger and sadness with hope.

Help me to rear my children
to be loving, responsible adults,
who feel confident and good about themselves.

Give me the courage to trust again.
And, if you can possibly manage it,
send someone kind and loving to share our lives.

And Then There Were Three

The house sold allowing us to move to Williamsburg in June. I found a nice rental house with a big back yard, and a job with Colonial Williamsburg. I enrolled Steven and Shannon in school. My friends became our extended family, and life settled into an almost normal routine. Then the child support payments stopped. When I called Buddy to find out why, his phone had been disconnected. Desperate, I called his boss in Roanoke. He had been fired after showing up for work drunk, and possessing illegal drugs. He had left town. Nobody knew where he had gone.

I tried not to panic. He would be in touch with the kids—he called every week—we would straighten this out. There must be an explanation. My pattern of denial continued.

He didn't call. Three weeks went by. Steven and Shannon were asking questions I couldn't answer. I started calling his old friends. Jackpot! He was in Phoenix, Arizona, staying with an army buddy, and playing guitar in a rock band. The friend gave me a number. I nervously dialed it. At that stage of my life, confrontation was not my strong suit. Buddy answered, loud music in the background. Surprised that I had found him, he laid it all on the line. No job. No plans to get a job. Needed some time for recreation. I had a job. I could support the kids.

Click. I hung up the silent phone in disbelief. Despite our personal animosity, I didn't think he would ever totally desert Steven and Shannon.

I was wrong. That would start a pattern that would continue for the next twenty years. I would get a child support order in Virginia. He would move to West Virginia, then to Georgia, then back to West Virginia, then back to Georgia. There was endless evasion and court battles.

Oh, he had jobs: mortgage banking; county government clerk; the list went on. Nothing lasted long enough for the child support office to pin him down for very long. The final blow: he became a minister, choosing small, cult-like churches who paid him in cash so there was no record of earnings. Worse than the money issue was the pain he inflicted on Steven and Shannon. It wasn't just the desertion. Far worse were the occasional plans he made to come and see them. They would get excited, and he wouldn't show—with no explanation. They coped by abandoning all expectations. Finally, when the child support arrearage was past $50,000, I did too. As they grew into their teens, he would occasionally write them letters, with threats of hell and damnation for a whole list of normal teenage activities, including listening to rock music. Shannon became fearful that he would show up on her doorstep one day to harass her in person. When he died of a massive heart attack in 2001, I felt no sadness, only relief that he couldn't hurt them anymore.

Despite the financial problems and personal disappointments, we built a good life in Williamsburg. We became members of Parents Without Partners, opening doors to fun activities with other single parent families, and showing us we weren't alone in our struggles. I was able to qualify for a low-interest loan, and buy a little townhouse in a small community with lots of other single moms and kids. I wrote this poem the day the divorce was final, after 2 years of battles.

Homemade Happiness

Sharon Dorsey, Steven Dorsey, Shannon Dorsey

My checking account balance is $23.
Today's chili will be tomorrow's tacos.
My car is a terminal senior citizen.
I'm afraid to open the bills that came in the mail today.
The heat pump sounds like it's full of marbles.
But the divorce papers are finally signed.
My nest is safe and warm.
My children are becoming real people who I like
and I am free.

Mothers/Fathers

When single mothers are fathers too,
we wonder...
are our children being cheated?

We can kick a soccer ball,
hostess a tea party for Barbie dolls,
carve a Pinewood Derby car.

We can cook pizza for a gang of twelve,
drive the kids to piano, Fife and Drum practice,
and chaperone the eighth grade dance.

We can work overtime to pay for vacations,
stay up late, finding money for a prom dress,
show no fear when the car dies.

We can provide stability in scary times,
offer a shoulder to lean on,
give out hugs for no reason at all.

But we still wonder...
...is it enough?
...are we enough?

Then cards arrive on Mother's Day
AND Father's Day,
thanking us for the Pinewood Derby car,
remembering the prom dress.

And we have our answer.

I worked two jobs for a couple of years: daytime at Colonial Williamsburg, and a sales job with Mary Kay Cosmetics, evenings and week-ends. When the Mary Kay business prospered, and I qualified to become a Sales Director with a company car, I took a deep, nervous breath and left Colonial Williamsburg. That change allowed me to work at home and, in addition, be available to the kids.

Steven and Shannon thrived in school. Steven was accepted into the Colonial Williamsburg Fife and Drum Corps. Shannon became a juvenile interpreter for Colonial Williamsburg, and a Colonial Dancer. They took piano lessons, and Shannon won a couple of junior high speech contests. They both participated in Model U.N., and my flexible job allowed me to chaperone their field trips. I wrote this poem after one of their competitions.

Reflections On The Model U. N.

They come from every state and territory.
They each represent a United Nations country.

They are urban and rural.
They are all unique, yet all alike.
They are idealistic and sarcastic.
They are confident and insecure.
They are graceful and awkward.
They are savvy and childlike.

They hover on the brink of adulthood.
They are the future leaders of our world.
We are in good hands.

Those Three Musketeers years flew by. When Steven's Junior Prom arrived, I couldn't believe he was almost grown. I wrote this poem on Prom Night, 1987. I would remember it with the same amazement when we were shopping for prom dresses for Shannon.

86

Time

Where does it go, the priceless time we lavish on trivia...
Where do they go, the precious children we carried and cuddled...
Where do we go, when they have flown to lives of their own...
Where is it written that life is graceful and serene...
Where is it hidden, the truth about living and loving...
Why don't they tell us...we create our own happily ever afters.

Epilogue: Steven and Shannon would continue their academic success, both working to put themselves through college, attaining Bachelor's and then Master's degrees, continuing to make me a proud Mom.

Above: Steven Dorsey
Junior Prom, 1987

Right: Shannon Dorsey
Junior Prom, 1991

At the very beginning of my single parenting years, I made a conscious decision to try and surround my children with people who I hoped would become an extended family for us.

It was obvious, even before the divorce was final, that their father was not going to be around. My Dad had died in 1974. My mother and siblings were in West Virginia.

But our *Sweet Adeline* and *Parents Without Partners* friends, along with my cousin Ginger, filled that void. They made Steven's and Shannon's lives, as well as mine, full and rich. I honor them with this poem.

Friendship

She stumbles.
The others support her until she can stand alone.

Another falls.
They pick her up and soothe her pain.

It is a joyful day.
They all share in the triumph.

One passes on to the next life.
The tears of those left behind heal the loss.

They have shared marriages, divorces, births, deaths.
They have celebrated in the sun and mourned in the shadows.

They are kindred souls, sisters and brothers of different mothers.
They are forever friends.

Ten Suggestions For A Fulfilling Life

From the day I became a single Mom, I worried about dying, and leaving my children alone. Logically, I knew they would be cared for and loved. I made those arrangements.

But what about their psychological and spiritual well-being? I felt compelled to leave them my personal truths. That desire to pass on the lessons I'd learned became the suggestions below.

1. Believe in something: a higher power, a spirit, nature, whatever you choose, but don't expect it to do life's work for you. Remember this little saying, "If it is to be, it's up to me."

2. Believe in yourself, and love yourself. You are unique and special, and there is no one else exactly like you.

3. Notice and respect the natural world around you. Smell the flowers, marvel at the creatures, plant trees, clean up debris, recycle. Pass on that reverence to your children and other people's children.

4. Find an occupation or avocation that you are passionate about. Make a difference in your world. You can do that by affecting one person or righting one wrong.

5. Love someone unconditionally: a child, a spouse, a friend, a lonely stranger. Unconditional love makes us powerful and joyful.

6. Nourish the soul: read, listen to music, study great art, create your own masterpiece. We cannot give to others, either in the workplace or at home, unless we continue to refill ourselves.

7. Broaden your world view by studying all the great religions and welcoming diversity into your circle. We will never have peace in the world until we learn to listen to each other. Practice tolerance and teach it to the next generation.

8. Take care of your body. Tone it, nourish it, and cherish it like the great instrument it is.

9. Never stop learning and searching for truth: about the universe and beyond, and about yourself.

10. Live your life as if you believed in karma, whether you do or not, assuming that what you put into the lives of others and the world, good or bad, will come back to you.

Footprints

The ghosts of vacations past walk with me today.
I step in my own footprints through
Cinderella's Castle to Tomorrow Land.
Everything is the same, yet nothing is the same.

The husband footprints next to mine are empty.
The little boy who held tight to Dumbo's ride
is now a tall, responsible teen.
The curly-haired toddler who played princess
has grown into one.

I walk in my own footprints, but I am not the same.
The old me waited for someone to take her hand
and lead her to happiness.
The new me braves unexplored territory
in search of her own rainbows.

The old me feared change.
The new me welcomes it, embraces it.
The old me leaned.
The new me can allow others to lean.

The ghosts of vacations past can rest in peace,
without regrets,
as the new spirits of freedom
fill the empty footprints and stride ahead.

Chapter 4

The Second Time Around

A Riddle Of Frogs And Princes

How many frogs does a single Mom
have to kiss to find a prince?

First, there was Jonathan,
a sophisticated and sexy engineer,
who was also a singer/actor,
and escorted me to plays and concerts.
But, alas, was committed
to being uncommitted.
Should have listened to my friends. GONE.

Next, I met Mark, a charismatic
Methodist minister, with great hair,
a booming bass voice, and impeccable manners.
But, alas, he didn't want his congregation
to know he had a girlfriend.
Should have dumped him after the first date.
SO Gone.

Doug was charming, with a sweet smile,
the successful manager of a tourist attraction,
who wrote novels in his spare time and left romantic poems under my
windshield wipers.
But, alas, alas, came with a secret wife.
Should never have accepted that first rose. Quickly, GONE.

By contestant #4, I had decided
princes were extinct, like dinosaurs.
Don didn't sing or dance
and was three inches shorter than me.
But, he was witty, brilliant, wanted to travel,
and fell madly in love with me and my children.
We loved each other passionately
and happily for twenty-five years.

So, how many frogs does it take to find a prince?
Doesn't matter, as long as you find him.

(The names, except for contestant #4, have been changed to protect the
rejected.)

Then There Was Don

In 1988, just when I had reached a time in my life when I was happy and didn't feel I needed a man in my life, Don arrived. We met on a blind date arranged by a mutual friend. I agreed to go to dinner with him to get her off my back. By the end of the evening, I knew he was different from all the other men I had known. He was interesting, traveled, smart, and funny. We shared an optimism about life. We had both moved away from organized religion but we believed in honesty and giving back to the world. We had similar stories to tell about past relationships: what we had learned from them, what we wanted in the future, what we didn't want. It was a rare conversation for a first date.

We had both been single for several years. Don, like me, had a busy life. He was retired from thirty-one years in the Air Force, and he owned a gymnastics studio. He liked to kayak, ski, and hike. My busyness stemmed from raising my kids, and building a business: all work and not much play. We didn't share the same hobbies, but we did share a value system, based loosely on the Buddhist philosophy of "think kind thoughts, do kind deeds." We felt safe being open with each other.

That was just the first evening. It was the beginning of twenty-five years of adventures -- traveling to places I'd dreamed about, climbing mountains, hiking in rainforests, and sleeping under the stars amidst Anasasi Indian ruins. During our many cross-country trips, I developed the same deep love of the southwest that Don had grown up with. He had been raised in Kansas City, Missouri but had spent summers in New Mexico. When he graduated from high school, he moved to Salt Lake City, Utah, to live with his uncle and aunt and attend college. Those years in the southwest had given him tremendous respect and affection for Native American culture and art. As we visited Native sites and museums, I grew to cherish my own Native American heritage even more.

When Don and I met, Steven was in college, and Shannon was in high school.

I didn't expect him to take on a parenting role, or them to encourage that role. But he did, and they did, and I watched, delighted. He became the male role model Steven had never had and he became the doting Dad that Shannon needed during those teen years. Don and I chaperoned her senior prom, and

Don shed father tears on her wedding day. He was Steven's best man when he wed Amy, the love of his life. When they gave us three grandchildren, he was the fun Pop-pa, playing games, and making them squeal with laughter. I have never stopped thanking the friend who refused to give up until I agreed to that first blind date.

L to R: Steven Dorsey, Sharon Dorsey, Don Frew, Shannon Dorsey
1996

Reflections

I used to think that happiness would come to one and all.
I used to think success was at each person's beck and call.
I used to think that love would always be there,
sure and strong.
I used to think my life would be as carefree as a song.

It took a lot of living and a lot of pain and strife,
for me to finally realize that I control my life.

You can't make me sad unless I choose for it to be.
You can't make me happy...
that must come from inside me.
You can't solve my problems...I must do that on my own
You can't give me peace of mind... I must find that alone.

But you can share your thoughts with me
and lighten both our loads.
And you can put your hand in mine
as we walk down the road.

If we can make the walls between us crumble with a smile,
then we can learn to trust and love
and make it all worthwhile.

Ate Out Again Today

I once saw a postcard in a gift shop with a picture of a pioneer woman in a sunbonnet, bending over a campfire in front of a Conestoga wagon. The caption was, *Ate out again today.* I can now somewhat relate to that woman. I just spent eight weeks eating out of a 22 ft. tin can on wheels, driven by a man who thinks he's a modern day Lewis and/or Clark.

The love of my life was retired from 31 years in the Air Force, wanted to travel, and go exploring. We had survived one cross-country tent camping trip. After several nights of sleeping out in 102 degree temperatures, I declared no more, unless he could find a tent with air conditioning and a bathroom. Our friends kept raving about RVing. So after several weeks of brainwashing, we succumbed. We bought the tin can on wheels. Before I could learn the words to Get Your Kicks on Rt. 66, we were on our way, somewhere.

On The Road...I had never seen Don so excited. I had gotten a little caught up in the hype myself. Our home away from home was cozy, with its tiny kitchen and minuscule bathroom. It was like playing house. Romantic and quaint, I thought.

I had a lot to learn.

My education began with the special dinner I planned for our first night on the road. We checked into the RV park, and I send Don out to have manly discussions about road maps and such with the other guys who had also been evicted. I set the table carefully, lit the candles, and turned my attention to the food. This was fun! I chopped all the veggies on my miniature cutting board, arranged all the ingredients for Don's favorite stir fry, and turned on the gas stove.

Nothing happened.

I tried again.

Nothing.

I yelled out the door, "Honey, would you turn on the gas?" He gave me one of those deer in the headlights looks. He had forgotten to fill the propane tank. I arranged the veggies artistically on plates, and Don declared it was the best dinner he'd ever eaten.

The next challenge was preparing our bed. Before leaving home, we had practiced creating a bed from the table top and cushions. That part was easy. Getting around the table (now the bed) was not so easy or painless. It resulted in bruised knees and shins. We eventually worked out a system for going to bed, and getting up. We undressed first, took turns in the bathroom, and then made the bed. The only glitch came when the one sleeping in the back needed to go to the bathroom in the middle of the night.

There was a bright side to the inconvenience. There could be no late night snacking, because we couldn't open the refrigerator door. I was sure I would be svelte by the time we returned home.

Invasion... The ants came onboard sometime during our second night on the road, and joined us for breakfast. Despite our best efforts to evict them, they remained steadfast across the country, surfacing for dinner, and disappearing when the food was gone. On the third day, they were joined by big, grey moths who emerged from the overhead vents. We hoped the moths would dine on the ants. We were disappointed because they had found something tastier in the vents. They would disappear during the day, only to fly out again when we turned on the ceiling fan in the evening. As we passed through field after field of Kansas corn and giant sunflowers, we kept looking back to be sure a swarm of hungry locusts wasn't trailing behind.

Kansas actually turned out to be our happy place. The ants and moths disembarked somewhere in the Sunflower State, probably from boredom, during the endless drive. They were never seen again. We're pretty sure they left of their own accord because we found no bodies when we cleaned the vents and the cabinets at our next stop.

Lost And Found... We spent a lot of time on the back roads. Consequently, we were sometimes lost, or as Mr. Lewis/Clark described it, in unexpected surroundings.

In New England, we followed a sign advertising maple syrup, and found ourselves on a dirt road. It was too narrow for turn-arounds, and seemed to go on and on to nowhere. After driving for nearly an hour, the road dead-ended at a deserted-looking farm with ramshackle barns and out-buildings. Disappointed, we were turning around to leave when a Santa Claus look-alike appeared from one of the barns. Smiling, he invited for us to join him. He was Norwegian, with a charming accent, and proceeded to take us on a tour of the farm, throwing in a visit to the horse barns. Inside one rickety barn was a spotless, stainless steel syrup-making operation.

On the Oregon coast, we found ourselves in unexpected surroundings again, bumping along a rocky road that narrowed to one lane, with thick bushes and trees on both sides of the road. There was nothing to do but follow it to its end. Just when we thought we were going to have to hike out for help, the road emerged from the trees and in the clearing was a white sand beach, wiped clean of every footprint. We spread our blanket on the sand, ate our sandwiches and watched the sinking sun finger-paint the sky in hues of palest pink to flaming orange. We sat in the sand, holding hands, until the last trace of rose faded from the sky. The seals barked goodnight as we climbed the hill to our home on wheels.

Patriotism Lives... We had no schedule as we wandered around the country, except we wanted to be in Salt Lake City for the 4th of July. Nobody does that family holiday better than our Mormon friends. There is a wonderful sameness about 4th of July parades.

...The high school band members, red-faced in 100-degree heat, still managed to high-step as they marched. Faithful band moms ran along side, spritzing the kids with water, and looked as if they need someone to spritz them too.

...The awkward, little girl dance troupes, with gangly legs and sparkly costumes, brandishing batons and toothless grins that turn parents and grandparents into lumps of loving goo.

...Acres of Boy and Girl Scouts, resplendent in uniforms plastered with patches and medals.

...Politicians, flashing winning smiles, aimed at gaining votes in the next election.

...Antique cars, filled with antique grandmas and grandpas, waving and throwing candy to the kids on the sidelines

....Papier-Mache floats, transporting radiant beauty queens in glittering crowns and fairytale gowns.

Two things were unusual in this parade...

...Dozens of Harley dudes and chicks on bikes, escorting a float filled with laughing kids, identified by a huge sign that read, Bikers Against Child Abuse.

...A van filled with Special Olympics athletes that got more applause than the politicians.

The best part of the parade, and the real reason I wanted to attend, was last—everyone in the crowd standing, hats off and hands over hearts, as Old Glory passed by, escorted proudly by the high school drill team, and followed by the Veterans of Foreign Wars, in faded uniforms and polished boots.

North To Alaska... The Al/Can Highway meanders to Alaska through some areas that look a little like Kansas, except wheat fields instead of corn. In the flat-lands, there are signs warning, Highway Serves as Emergency Airstrip. We came down over a hill, and screeched to a stop. A small airplane had made an emergency landing on the narrow, two-lane road. The pilot had lost fuel, and luckily, found the road in time. Don was an experienced airplane mechanic. He found the leak, repaired it and, as the Mounties arrived, we headed on to Alaska--my mechanic sporting a hero's grin.

Don Frew, repairing plane on way to Alaska

Many thousand miles, and many adventures later, I am home, suntanned, ten pounds lighter, and rattling around in a townhouse that suddenly seems huge. Last night, I couldn't sleep. I crept out to the R. V., crawled into my table/bed, and fell asleep instantly-- to dream of maple syrup, orange sunsets, and Conestoga wagons.

Lessons I Learned On My Summer Vacation

Vacations used to leave me with memories of beaches, mountains, and shoe boxes full of faded snapshots. A 90-day, 12,000-mile adventure across America and British Columbia, from Atlantic to Pacific, left Don and me with vivid mental snapshots of the heart of our land. In my search for a definition of who we Americans have become, I found the good, the bad, and the ugly. But I found our heartbeat strong, and full of pride.

I also learned some unexpected lessons.

Patriotism Is Alive...I learned the Pennsylvania Dutch and Amish farm families around Lancaster Co., PA. know how to celebrate the 4th of July. Small flags wave in neat rows across their lawns. Red, white, and blue bunting decorates their porches and advertises their patriotism. They gather together for ice cream socials and picnics, and their children know the true meaning of this most important holiday. Our Founding Fathers would be proud.

Corn, Corn, Everywhere... The cornfields of Kansas look very much like those of Iowa and Nebraska. But South Dakota rewards the weary traveler with shining fields of golden sunflowers, stretching for miles into the horizon.

R.V. Parks And Art Galleries...R.V. parks are as varied as the vehicles parked there. Our overnight homes ranged from lush parks to concrete pads. My favorite was a small, quiet campground in Grants Pass, Oregon. It was an outdoor art gallery, with whimsical sculptures and wood carvings, all crafted and shared with much pride by the owner.

If You Don't Like The Weather, Just Wait...I learned to appreciate 55 degrees in Washington and Oregon after 105 degrees in Iowa and Nebraska. I even learned to like cold showers in unheated bathhouses inhabited by tiny lizards.

Well, almost.

Goodness And Honesty Still Exist... There are nice people in Lewiston, Montana, who not only repaired our ailing transmission at a fair price, but loaned us their personal car, packed us a picnic lunch, and send us off with a map to explore their little town while we were waiting for the repairs to be finished. News travels fast in a small town. Everyplace we went, we were treated as special guests.

Yes, There Really Is A Corn Palace... In Mitchell, S.D., there is a

101

magnificent palace covered in corn kernels and multi-hued corn husks. It is refurbished every year with a new design. The townspeople work for weeks to create this remarkable building. It is an expression of pride in their farming community.

All Men Are Created Equal—Not Always... Sadly, many Native Americans on the Sioux, Crow and Navaho reservations still live in squalor and poverty.

Rusting car bodies litter the parched yards of small, square-box houses in need of paint. Faded laundry bakes on sagging lines in the boiling sun. Jobs are difficult to find, and young people leave school too soon. Drug and alcohol addiction are commonplace.

A lucky few escape to college. Some return to the reservation to help the hopeless. Such is the case of a beautiful Lakota Sioux woman in Chamberlain, South Dakota. She grew up in a Catholic boarding school for orphans because her parents had more children than they could feed. She graduated, went on to college, and is now back home. We met her in the small art gallery she has opened to help market the crafts of her people. She also works as a housemother in the orphanage where she grew up. She is teaching the Sioux children to have pride in their heritage, and she is making a difference in their lives.

Family Reunions Are All The Same... Whether they are held in a city park or on an Indian reservation, family reunions are a lot alike. Our new Lakota friend invited us to attend a Pow Wow, which is a family reunion, but with drums and dancers. We were greeted by young teens on ponies, racing over the gently sloping grasslands. As we wandered around, we saw older teens in jeans with spiked hair, looking bored, and above it all. Giggling little girls behaved like giggling little girls everywhere. Grandmothers with braids, dressed in long, brightly-colored dresses gossiped while their men gathered in small circles, smoking, and not talking much. Barefoot babies slept on patchwork quilts on the grass, guarded by proud mothers. The haunting cry of a flute filtered through the trees, carried on the wind. The unrelenting beat of the drums echoed across the plains as these special people, the First People of our land, proclaimed their ancestral pride with their dances and their regalia of deerskin and feathers.

The Impossible Takes A Little Longer... My visit to Crazy Horse Mountain in South Dakota taught me that the human spirit is indomitable. Some people refuse to give up their dreams, despite seemingly insurmountable obstacles. Case in point --

Korczak Ziolkowski, a Polish sculptor. He spent 50 years carving a gigantic figure of Chief Crazy Horse into the granite of the Black Hills as a tribute to the native people. He died in 1982 with only the head of the carving completed. But his wife, children, and grandchildren are carrying on the dream. The completed figure of the Sioux chief, seated on his horse, arm outstretched, will be 563 feet tall, larger than the presidential figures on Mt. Rushmore.

Pride In Stone... At Mt. Rushmore, I discovered I can still be awe-struck. The first sight of the mountain makes your heart jump in surprise. As you approach the park by vehicle, it is suddenly there: so visible, so accessible, and so grand. We've all seen photos, but none do justice to this masterpiece. When I visited the crude studio of the creator, Gutson Borglum, and looked at the original models, then out the window at the real thing, I was humbled at the artist's genius and vision. He felt such pride in being an American, that he wanted to give something back. He gave us a treasure.

Independence Begins Early... In Wyoming, there is a massive basalt mountain, called Devil's Tower, that rises 867 feet above its 1,000-foot diameter base. Huge boulders litter the hillside leading up to the tower. They present a tricky challenge for climbers. I gave up after a short distance, and climbed onto a big rock to watch. Sharing my perch was a Native American family, attentively watching three young teenagers scramble to the base, pose for the standard triumphant photo, and then carefully make their way down. The three were agile, and made the trip up and back very quickly. But the family continued to watch two other figures, descending slowly. I learned it was a mother, and her five-year-old daughter. I watched with them as the mother took one small step at a time, and instructed the little girl to follow in her footsteps. The husband/father watched nervously as the pair neared the bottom. He met them, and reached out to lift the beaming child over the last big boulder. The mother stopped him and I heard her say, "No, let her find her way. She must feel pride in herself."

Lively Ghost Towns... As we continued through Wyoming, I discovered that sagebrush can be as boring as Kansas cornfields. But here, the names of the cities kept my imagination awake and working overtime: Sundance, Buffalo, Billings and Bighorn evoked images of Indian battles and Gold Rush towns. My mind's eye filled the sagebrush with boisterous life.

What If?... In Montana, I was surprised to learn that eleven Indian tribes live on reservations in this state: the Crow, Blackfeet, Flathead, Northern Cheyenne, Assiniboine, Sioux, Gros Ventre, Chippewa, Cree, Salish, and Kootenai. One has to wonder how different our crowded, polluted land would be today if these eco-conscious people had been allowed to remain on their own lands, caring for them, and about them.

From Shocking To Historic... The tiny town of Wallace, Idaho illustrates how time can put an entirely different prospective on an event, changing the scandalous into the quaint. This small, silver mining town, population 1,010, is listed in its entirety in the Historical Register. The original buildings now house museums. The most interesting is the Bordello Museum, telling the story, without apology, of the ladies of the evening. Their patrons often left in a hurry, leaving behind everything from their long johns to bags of groceries. The museum displays many of these fascinating objects. At the end of the tour, we were informed that the brothel began operation in 1895 and closed in 1989.

Yes, that's right, 1989.

Priceless Trivia... Kansas and Missouri filled my journal with trivia jewels.

...The Barbed Wire Museum in LaCrosse, Kansas, features more than 500 different types of the prickly stuff. Who knew??

...Only Rome, Italy has more fountains than Kansas City, Missouri. It also claims the dubious honor of having built America's first shopping center.

...It was once illegal to serve ice cream on cherry pie in Kansas. Nobody seemed to know why.

...If you're having a less than wonderful family vacation and want to lose the kids for a while, the corn maze in Buhler, Kansas is the place to go. They do, however, insist that you collect them before dark.

A Cheese Lovers Delight... In Tillamook, Oregon, I watched my favorite food being made at the largest cheese factory in the state. Unfortunately, I learned that watching those delicious cheeses being made doesn't alter the hand to waist calorie progression.

Is This Really Progress? While spending several sun-filled days cruising the blue-green waters of Lake Powell in Utah, I reconfirmed my conviction that progress is not always better. High on a sheer, rocky cliff in the middle of the lake, is one of the few remaining Anasasi ruins in the area. I grieved for all the beauty and history lost when the other ruins were flooded by the Glen Canyon Dam. True, it is a beautiful recreation area, enjoyed by boaters, but in the process, we have deliberately destroyed the story of a civilization.

The Raven's Lament

They vanished seven hundred years ago,
the ancient ones, the gatherers.
They told stories of their lives
on cave walls and picture rocks.
They left pottery and tools in their granaries
and rocky hillside houses.
But we flooded their homes
and forever erased their history.
Now we drive powerboats through the waters
covering their hunting grounds,
and only the circling ravens knows their secrets,
proclaiming their stories in their haunting laments.

Paradise Found... On the Oregon coast, I delighted in deserted beaches, wiped clean of every footprint, reminding me of something important I'd forgotten in my busy life at home. Solitude is good for the soul. Forever etched in my memory is a sunset, so breathtakingly beautiful, I thought, if I were to die here, in this place, in this perfect moment, it would be OK. Everyone should have a moment like that.

Hooray For Mysteries!... In the Oregon Vortex, in Gold Hill, Oregon, I found that even the most astute scientific minds can't explain everything. In the *House of Mystery,* balls roll uphill, short people appear taller and vice-versa. Engineers have conducted over 14,000 experiments and can only explain the phenomenon as a whirlpool of invisible energy.

It's A Small World... In a little community, just inside the California state line, I was reminded that sometimes things happen the way they are intended. We passed a tiny Native American craft shop, half hidden in the middle of a lily field. We quickly did one of our now-expert U-turns (due to a lot of practice. Inside, I found treasure. During the trip, I had been searching for just the right jewelry for my mother of the bride dress for daughter Shannon's Cherokee wedding, which would take place when we returned. I described my dress and the owner of the shop, a Tolala Indian, said his wife could make the jewelry for me. A look around provided all the other things I needed for the ceremony: a wedding vase, baskets for the potlatch gifts, and wonderful hand-crafted feather boxes for the two Cherokee officiants. When I pulled out one of my Mary Kay Cosmetics business cards to provide a mailing address for the jewelry, the man smiled and said, "My wife is a *Mary Kay Beauty Consultant*, too." I left, knowing I had made two new friends.

Why Are We Cutting Old Growth Trees?... The towering redwoods in Northern California taught me a valuable lesson in humility. How insignificant our life span is compared to the 2000-year life span of the great trees. What stories they could tell, and how sad that so few remain. The mountains above the coast have been ravaged by loggers. That's a lesson I wish I hadn't learned.

Kayaking In The San Juans... In the waters surrounding Orcas Island in the San Juan Islands, off the coast of Seattle, I learned that going out kayaking for the first time can be daunting. The first lesson was getting into the unfamiliar gear. The second lesson was how to step into the boat, wearing the gear, without tipping it over. The third lesson was how to handle the paddle without whacking my friend/instructor, Mike, in the head. After all that, it was smooth gliding through the clear, blue water, UNTIL, I heard a horn in the distance and looked over my shoulder to see a three-stories-tall ferry, headed straight for us. We paddled like crazy for shore and all ended well.

106

Killer Whales I Met... Orcas Island is named for the gentle 7-ton giants who reside year 'round in the waters surrounding the San Juan Islands. There are over 100 killer whales in three pods (families who roam miles through the islands to feed and play. Each Orca has been given a name by researchers who have been working in the area for years, and each has been identified as a member of a specific family. On a foggy morning, we bundled up and headed off on one of the small research boats in search of Orcas. Actually, they found us, peeping black shiny noses out of the water to rub on the sides of the boat, then swim off to perform amazing acrobatics for us. By the end of the day, we had been visited by all three pods—an incredible sight. The scientists were as amazed as us, confessing they had never seen all three pods in one location—a once in a lifetime adventure.

Mother Nature's Beauty And Wrath... Two separate day-hikes in the Seattle, Washington area, gave me perfect examples of those two things—the incredible beauty and quiet peace of the forests and cliffs of Mt. Ranier vs. the catastrophic aftermath of Mt. St. Helen's fury. Looking across that vast wasteland at acres of downed trees, like match sticks in the distance, brought home the reality of nature's power. I kept remembering that old cliché: Don't mess with Mother Nature.

Man-Made Disaster... Olympic National Park in Washington State is a wonderland of deep green rain forests and gigantic trees. But timbering is taking a terrible toll on those forests, and the aftermath washes up on the beaches near the park at Ocean Shores. How amazing to see all those skeletons of trees past.

Revenge On Litterers... As we visited our beautiful state and national parks, it became obvious that we have become a nation of slobs. Litter is everywhere, often on the ground near a trash can. One woman, who parked beside us at a visitor center and emptied her ashtray on the ground by her car, may think twice before doing it again. When she went inside, leaving her white convertible top down, we returned the contents of her ashtray to her (and beat a hasty retreat).

Any City, U.S.A.... The biggest lesson of the trip came as no surprise. We have become a land of Any City, U. S. A., with Walmarts and Dairy Queens stretching end to end from Atlantic to Pacific. But if you take the time to get off the beaten interstate, and drive the back roads, you will discover a distinctive regional flavor in each small town, including imaginative welcome and farewell signs. My favorite was in Shady Cove, Oregon. It proclaimed in huge letters, "THANKS FOR COMING...LOVE YA!"

That sums up my feelings about this unique melting-pot my Cherokee ancestors called Turtle Island and we call America.

LOVE YA!

No Greater Love... At a museum in Prescott, Arizona, I learned the story of a Yavapi Indian village of 1700 men, women and children who were forced to walk 180 miles from the Verde Valley of Arizona to San Carlos, California in the winter of 1875 when their land was confiscated for settlers arriving from the East. Their struggles and suffering inspired this ballad.

No Greater Love

They came in the darkness, forcing us from our blankets.
The Blue Coats came, with loud voices and angry eyes,
herding us, like cattle, from our wickiups, into the night.
They told us we must leave our land
and go to another place.
They told us to gather our blankets and corn,
and prepare to walk for many days.

"Leave me here!" Grandmother cried. "I cannot walk.
Let me die here in the shadow of the Sacred Mountain."
"No!" Grandfather said, "I will not leave you."
As the Blue Coats went from hut to hut with their torches,
Grandfather readied a large basket.

He strapped it to his back, and stooped down.
Grandmother climbed in, her legs dangling.
They journeyed many days,
Grandfather carrying Grandmother in her basket.
Others offered to help, but he bore his burden proudly.

Father Winter brushed the trees with white.
Grandfather struggled against the wind.
Grandmother whimpered from the cold.
He tried to walk faster,
but they fell behind the others.

Grandfather stumbled and couldn't get up.
Grandmother crawled from the basket,
and they huddled beneath a tree.
Father Winter covered them with a soft blanket of snow.
They drifted off to sleep, hands clasped.

Other stragglers, coming up the trail, found them.
Gently, they wrapped them in blankets,
and hoisted them onto their backs.
They fought their way up and over the last steep ridge.
Below, dozens of tiny lights shimmered like fireflies.

Reverently, they carried the old ones
down the hill into the valley.
They were welcomed and warmed
by the fires of their friends.
They were fed and given a place of honor at the campfire.
Grandfather smiled at Grandmother,
dozing in her warm blanket.
They had survived to see the new land.

Land Of The Free And Home Of The Brave

When did we become a land of Any City, U.S.A.,
with shopping malls and parking lots
where antelope once played.

Who decided we should harvest all the old growth trees,
home to nesting birds and busy hives of buzzing bees?

Where, in writing, does it say, that progress is the best--
here and there should be a park, and overcrowd the rest?

Who thinks that we should trash the land,
the heavens and the sea?
No one speaks up, accepts the blame. Its left to you and me.

The attitude is that we aren't the keeper of our brother.
Look out for number one without concern for one another.

We share this ship, this Mother Earth,
suspended high above.
We can't survive or prosper here, unless we learn to love.

Love creatures, large and small, who dwell upon this land.
Love trees, and fresh clean air, and mountains that are grand.

For what we love, we will protect and nurture till days end.
And then, perhaps, our home, the earth,
will slowly start to mend.

Timeless Moment

Listen long enough
to the wind in the canyon,
and you will hear
echoes of songs,
whispers of stories,
silence in the waiting space
that is empty of life,
yet brimming with ghosts
of thousand year struggles
in a deserted landscape-
a weather-scape of sun and storm,
an eternity of dawns and sunsets,
a time-scape of life past.

Don Frew, Sharon Dorsey
Grand Canyon
2006

111

Powwow
(Homecoming)

Fancy Dancers twirl around the grassy arena,
feathers flying, a swirl of scarlet, turquoise and yellow.

Women in buckskin and beaded moccasins circle,
shawl-covered arms outstretched,
butterflies in slow motion.

Jingle Dress Dancers add treble to the bass of the drums,
their skirts, the instrument,
their undulating bodies, the artist.

Prairie Grass Dancers stealthily track unseen beasts,
brandishing bows and arrows
in an age-old fight for survival.

Painted faces reach upward
to the sunlight of the Great Spirit.
Native hearts reach backward, connecting to ancestors.

And beneath it all, the compelling pulse of the drums
pounds out the timeless heartbeat of my people.

Moving Mania

Statisticians tell us we are a mobile society. In 2006, Don and I joined the statistics. We packed and moved our two households, and survived it with our sense of humor mostly intact. Lots of people combine their belongings and nestle in together. But when two collectors decide to stop traveling and nest, it's a big deal. We did not make this decision to merge, quickly or rashly. We thought about it for seventeen years, while accumulating stuff.

We were determined to find a house big enough for all of our combined treasures. Much to our surprise, we did find the perfect house. We took a couple of deep breaths, signed the contract, and put our two houses on the market. That's an adventure worthy of its own story someday—maybe a book on how to sell two houses quickly without losing your sunny disposition, or running down your realtor with his own SUV.

Our first thought, when we started packing, was to beg for help from our family. But they had seen our houses. Then we thought of our loyal friends; It was strange—each had commitments or travel plans. One even went so far as to schedule an operation. But there was one friend, Janie, who was in a martyr mood, and volunteered. That woman deserves to win the lottery. She hung in there through all the packing plus four moving days. It took four separate days, with two moving vans each day, to transport the belongings from our two houses to the wonderful new home in the wilds of James City County.

Don also had a 2,200 sq. ft. detached workshop, packed floor to ceiling with more stuff. When the movers came to give us an estimate, they glanced into the workshop (it wasn't possible to walk through it) and just shook their heads. The conclusion was, there's not enough money in your bank account to tempt us to undertake that mess. They worded it more kindly but the message was clear.

Highly offended, Don huffed and puffed, and declared he would move the contents of the workshop himself. Our household goods were delivered in July. Thanksgiving week, he finally moved the last load from the workshop into his new garage. He filled it, and three storage buildings. To his credit, the throw-away piles for the trash truck were as tall as the workshop, and probably sent those poor guys into early retirement.

July to Thanksgiving was spent with our boxes. In the beginning, there were so many, we couldn't get to our brand-new bed in our brand-new bedroom. We had to camp out in the guest room where we had a single path from the door to the bed—just one side of the bed. If one of us had to get up in the night, the other one either had to get up too, or suffer being climbed over.

I was quite naive in estimating the amount of time it would take to unpack, and find homes for all the stuff in those boxes. I thought a couple of weeks. At the end of two weeks, we still hadn't found our underwear, or the coffee pot.

Fortunately, those friends who were conveniently busy when we were packing, must have suffered from guilt, or maybe they were genuinely concerned for our health and sanity. Whatever, the result was lots of great food, cooked and ready to eat, the type neighbors provide for a funeral. That description was not totally inappropriate, for there were days when we were close to killing each other as we negotiated what would go where.

In any move, there is at least one item that simply won't fit anyplace. In our case, it was a grandiose painting of a long-forgotten ancestor. We didn't have the heart to throw him away, but the pompous-looking old gentleman is probably turning in his grave if he knows his portrait hangs in our pantry, diligently guarding the potatoes and onions.

Lost items are another problem. Shoes wander off easily, but unfortunately, never as a pair, so I made my first trip to the grocery store in one brown loafer and one black ballet slipper. Silverware, too, has a flighty disposition, hiding, only to materialize later in the bread box, or happily entwined in my best cashmere sweater.

Don and Janie both denied responsibility for that packing blunder, as do I, so I have to assume that Nobody did it. Nobody made a lot of strange packing decisions. Don's favorite suit couldn't be found when we emptied the wardrobe boxes. It turned up around Halloween, folded neatly in the bottom of a box labeled Garden Tools. Our first Christmas in our new home was magical. All the boxes were gone (or permanently hidden) and all of our treasures were stowed in their places. We walked around smiling a lot at the wonder of it all.

Those children, (remember, the ones who were too chicken to come home and help us pack), gathered at our new house during the holidays. It was definitely a case of shock and awe. They admitted to serious doubts that the old folks could bring order from all that chaos.

We had terrific visits. As each child left, they received a large package, beautifully wrapped, and tied with a gigantic bow. They were instructed not to open it until they were safely back home. I wish we could have seen their faces as they opened the boxes containing all the junk they had left in our respective attics, plus a few extra things we didn't want that we just threw in, for fun. We waited for the phone to ring. So far, no one has called to comment on their special gift, but I'm checking incoming parcels carefully.

Don Frew, Sharon Dorsey
First Christmas in new home
Williamsburg, VA
2006

The moral of this story is: If you have been waiting for the right time to merge with the person you love, get on with it. It was worth all the headaches to have those shared sunsets on warm summer nights, and brisk walks together on frosty autumn mornings.

One last piece of advice—find a really BIG house so you can escape from each other when you can't stand one more minute of togetherness. Above all, have a yard sale **BEFORE** you move, not after. You'll save enough money on storage buildings to purchase a hot tub for the deck.

Sharon And Don's Incredibly Happy Wedding

It was a rainy, dreary day on Tuesday, April 8, 2008, so Don and I decided to brighten it up by getting married. We thought it was a fitting way to celebrate our twenty years of togetherness.

First, we searched our closets for something red to wear, because it was, indeed, a red-letter day. Then we drove to the courthouse and got our license. Don tried to convince the clerk to give us a senior discount, but our AARP cards were of no benefit. We had to pay the full price. Then he called Steven to ask for my hand. With much pomp and circumstance, he said, "I'll take your Mom off your hands if you'll spring for the license fee. AND, I think I'll need a monthly stipend because I'm sure she'll be high maintenance." Steve agreed, even offering to pay for the reception. He suggested *Hardee*s but Don insisted on an upgrade to *Burger King*. The man had class.

The next step was to find someone to marry us. The licensing office gave us the name of a Marriage Commissioner (whatever that is). We called. He was available. We decided on 7:30 at our house.

We called Shannon at work and asked if she could be there at 7:30, dressed in red, of course. She was so excited, she said, "I can leave work now, if you want." I got the feeling my kids were happy to marry me off.

In between all the wedding stuff, we had to fit in some Mary Kay deliveries, a doctor appointment for Don, and a trip to the bank. As we were driving from errand to errand, we called a few friends who lived close by, told them to come in their blue jeans, wearing red, and show up at 7:30 for this momentous occasion. They were all speechless, but agreed to come.

At 4 p.m., we finally arrived home. Along the way, we had decided we probably should feed these people something for showing up on such short notice. But what? Don suggested peanut butter and jelly sandwiches, his favorite food. I insisted on equal time for my favorite food, cheesecake. So we set the dining room table with platters of peanut butter sandwiches, cheesecake, and crystal stemware (for the sparkling cider toast). Steven had send a beautiful basket of yellow and white daisies that had arrived while we were gone. It was the perfect table centerpiece. Shannon brought gorgeous flowers too, pink and yellow, so they decorated the buffet. Don presented me with a dozen red roses, and they adorned the coffee table in the living room where the ceremony would be performed.

We quickly did what Shannon calls the *flight of the bumblebee*, which is tidying up by flying around, and stuffing things in drawers and closets, etc. Don is quite experienced at this, so he cleared more area than me, and still had time to make his special peanut butter and jelly sandwiches. Between us, it all got done, with much laughter and anticipation.

Our friends were wonderful. They all came, some early, with extra food. The table filled up with casseroles, salad, salsa and chips, and a cake. Everybody came in their jeans, and a red something, as instructed. They even brought cards and presents. We were amazed.

At 7:30, we all gathered in the living room with Mr. Gilley, who wore a red tie. Shannon called Steven and held the phone up so he, Amy, and granddaughter Adaline, could hear the nuptials. (That was before we all had Skype or Face Time.) Don wanted to assure Steven that we really had gone through with it. Mr. Gilley gave a wonderful little opening speech about

marriage, which he had written himself. It was lovely. He said, "Do you...?" We said, "I do." He said, "I now pronounce you..." We kissed. Everybody cried and applauded and hugged everybody else. Then we ate and laughed until all the food was gone, including ALL the peanut butter sandwiches.

You'll notice Don is in his Halloween bear claw slippers. I didn't notice till halfway through the ceremony. I nearly laughed out loud and ruined the whole thing. That's my wonderful husband – going for the entertainment factor, even at his own wedding.

Don Frew
Making the outdoors more beautiful

A Valentine Thank You To My Husband

...For loving me, flaws and all.

...For giving me emotional security,
   for the first time in my life.

...For valuing me,
   so I could learn to value myself.

...For opening doors to fun and adventure,
   and teaching me how to play again.

...For taking me to the exotic places
   I've always dreamed about.

...For sharing knowledge,
   and life experience with me.

...For loving and helping my children,
   and giving them a positive father image.

...For giving me the perfect home, and
   welcoming family and friends into it.

...For gardening and planting flowers to make the
   outside of our home as beautiful as the inside.

I appreciate this special life we have together,
and I love you on this Valentine's Day and
every day.

Gypsy   2/14/11

Nobody Told Me

Nobody told me, when I was fifty or even when I was sixty,
that aging into my golden years might be a little tricky.

I pictured quiet evenings by the fire,
my love and I reading to each other,
sonnets, mysteries, the Times,
and all the Harry Potter novels, finally.
Nobody told me, I wouldn't be able to read the small print,
he would refuse to wear his hearing aids,
and sitting would give us backaches.

I envisioned more years of flying away
to our favorite secluded island,
and lots more cross-country adventures in our faithful RV.
Nobody told me, someday passengers would carry bombs
in their underpants, and gas would climb to $4 a gallon
in an RV that only gets six miles per gallon.

I was sure our children and grandchildren would be nearby,
and we would gather for Norman Rockwell-like birthdays
and Sunday dinners.
Nobody told me, they would develop careers
taking them far away, to raise families
that I would mostly visit via I Phone or I Pad.

I assumed my love and I would have that fairytale ending,
sitting on the porch at sunset, holding hands,
living happily ever after.
Nobody told me, someday a doctor would tell us a rare, incurable cancer,
caused by his exposure to Agent Orange in Vietnam,
would end the fairy tale.

As I watched other people face terminal illnesses,
I was positive I couldn't possibly be that brave.
Nobody told me, my love and I would sit in the car,
outside the doctor's office, and say to each other, dry-eyed,
"We are going to live our lives, for as long as we can."

I still feared every moment would be filled with the burdens of dying,
the rush to complete bucket lists,
and say all those profound things that needed to be said.
Nobody told me, most days would be filled with ordinary things--
planting flowers, eating ice cream at bedtime, fuming over politics,
all inter-woven with oncology visits.

Then the feared verdict came - acute leukemia,
no more treatment options, two weeks.
Again, we looked into each other's eyes and said,
"We are going to live our lives, till the end."
Nobody told me the pain of those two weeks
would be punctuated with so much laughter,
as loved ones came to tell funny stories, give hugs and say,
"Thank you for sharing our lives."

One day, watching the amazing parade,
I flashed back to a realization from earlier in our year,
that every moment spent stressing about tomorrow,
steals an irretrievable moment from today.
Nobody told me how freeing that simple truth would be.

(In loving tribute to my husband, Donald Frew,
who flew away to explore other realms on March 8, 2013.)

Saying Goodbye...

All the things I can't say out loud without crying...
You are not leaving me with lots of things to handle. Please stop worrying.
You are leaving me with a beautiful home filled with memories of our life together...
...the living room where you married me in your bear claw slippers.
...the family room filled with treasures from our many wonderful trips.
...our gorgeous yard where you spent so many hard-working hours.
...the bedroom where I spent magical hours in your arms.
...the dining room where we ate, drank, and made merry with our family and friends.

I WILL MISS...
...talking to you, about anything and everything,
...holding your hand when I go to sleep,
...waking up, just to listen to you breathe, and falling back to sleep, feeling safe,
...laughing with you over the silliest things,
...being handsomely escorted anyplace I wanted to go (even those rotten movies, like Snow Days, remember?)
I will even miss the disagreements. They are a part of life,
plus, they sharpened my debating skills.

I MAY NOT MISS...
...riding in your truck,
...cooking squash and onions,
...that garage filled with stuff, stuff, and more stuff.

I REMEMBER...
...cooking breakfast at 3a.m. on our first get-away together, because that's when we woke up.
...watching the whales play at sunset on a black sand beach in Hawaii.
...hiking through the wildflower meadows in B.C.
...arriving at Cooper Island, British Virgin Islands, a few days after 9/11, and wondering how so much ugliness and so much beauty could exist in the same world.
...picking wild blackberries on Orcas Island in British Columbia.
...chaperoning Shannon's senior prom. You were so handsome and I felt

like your princess in my long gown.

...watching you comfort my mother so lovingly during one of her hysterical moments, calling her *Mom* and telling her everything would be all right.

 ...seeing you standing beside Steven at his wedding, so handsome in your dress uniform, the proudest of Dads, and wondering, as I have so often over the years, how I could have been lucky enough to find a father like you for my children. I wished for you - and there you were.

...our first driving trip out West, when we packed the car with everything we could possibly ever need and camped in the little tent until the last night, when you surprised me with the VIP suite on the Air force base. What a way to win a girl over.

...so many nights in so many beautiful places, when the best part of the day was closing the door and going into your arms. Nothing we saw or did was more special than those moments.

...snuggling under the stars on the windjammer, wondering what adventure the next morning would bring.

...our first night in our house, sleeping in the guest room surrounded by tall stacks of boxes with just a path to get out and go to the bathroom. And that day, many months later, when the boxes were finally gone and we could just sit and look around and smile.

...all the Christmases, the birthdays, and the ordinary days. I never took for granted the small miracles like being able to wake up together in our very own home.

...the novelty, when we first started dating and through all the years together, of always having something to look forward to.

...the sheer joy I have always felt when you would suddenly, for no reason, throw your arms around me, as if you were just so uncontrollably happy with us, with life.

...so many moments in a rich life together, tied with ribbons of love and respect and appreciation.

I will always remember.

Your Gypsy   Jan. 2013

The Last Love Letter

Love,

If I should ever leave you to go along the silent
way, do not speak of me with tears,
but laugh and talk of me as if I were beside you.

And when you see a bird or hear a song I loved,
please do not let the thoughts of me be sad.

For I am loving you, just as I always loved you.

There were so many things I still wanted to do,
so many things still to say to you.

Remember that I did not fear death.

It was leaving you that was so hard to face.

We cannot see what lies beyond but this I know
I loved you so, my dear,
'twas heaven here on earth with you.

Don

The Desk

The roll-top looms large and intimidating in the small,
sunny room. My husband, Don, saved everything.
The endless minutia of life oozes from every orifice.

I have avoided this painfully personal treasure trove
for months, too traumatized by his death to tackle it.
Today, I dive in, starting with the boxes beneath the desk...

...Military records going back to 1949, the beginning of a
31-year career in the Air Force, culminating in his
promotion to Colonel in 1968 and retirement in 1980.
I watch him age in the promotion photos,
wondering if I would have liked that stern young man.

...Divorce papers from the early 80's,
attached to a neatly printed and numbered note,
listing the pros and cons of ending a marriage.

...An envelope, entitled, *old friends and old flames,*
filled with photos of smiling couples, kayaking, skiing--
Don looking relaxed, happy, like the man I met in 1988.

...More papers - financial statements from the purchase
of our dream house, a much lamented speeding ticket for
going 45 in a 35 mile zone, his first ticket, unusual for
someone who built and raced cars in his youth.

I sort the stacks into Save, Shred, Recycle, and Toss.

Then I tackle the drawers...

...Post cards of our trips to Mexico, Hawaii, British Virgin
Islands, and road trips to 49 of the 50 states, a mini
travelogue of our 25 years together.

...Glasses, magnifiers, hearing aids he refused to wear, love
letters from children, from me, a *welcome to the world* note for
a new grandchild, scrawled on an envelope.

...Sticky notes with philosophical and political musings,
cartoons, irreverent jokes, his favorite saying,
Life's uncertain. Eat your dessert first,
printed in big letters on a yellow paper napkin.

The sun is sinking low in the sky and shadows fill the room
as I wearily open the last drawer.

...Medical records, a year of tests, oncology visits and blood
transfusions, aimed at controlling a relentless enemy,
spawned by exposure to Agent Orange in Vietnam.

The desk is empty now, the messy, overflowing piles
neatly contained. Task complete, like the messy,
overflowing, uncontained life, also now complete.

As I stand up to turn out the light,
a crumbled piece of paper flutters to the floor.
It says, "I wouldn't trade tomorrow
for the best yesterday I ever lived."

Hard to lose a man like that.

Chapter 5

Love Goes On...The Next Generations

Renewal

They cross the street slowly,
twelve of them,
tiny heads up,
flat feet planted firmly
on the pavement.
Mother goose leads the parade,
Father goose guards the rear.
Cars stop.
Drivers relax.
Everyone smiles.
A tiny moment
in a busy day,
a reminder
of why we're here.

Life renewing life.

Happy Graduation Day!!!!!

Shannon went back to college after a traumatic divorce, and completed her Bachelor's Degree while working full-time and taking care of a houseful of adopted pets. We had a big celebration when she graduated and I read this poem at the party.

There is so much we want to say...
Homework, and housework and job work too,
You did it, you did it! Hooray for you!

Those A's paid off, as you will see,
as you frame your new Bachelor's Degree.

We are so proud. We expected no less.
We knew all along you'd do your best.

So take a deep breath and take time to play,
with your furry children and new love, A. J.

Your future is yours, to mold and to choose,
to pursue your dreams, to follow the clues.

It's just the beginning of bright, shining days,
with all those who love you and your special ways.

In the words of Seuss, our favorite Doc...
Will you succeed? You will indeed!

7/7/11

PROUD MOM NOTE: Shannon's now working on her Master's Degree and will graduate in 2017, with A. J. and all the family cheering her on.

My Daughter, The Animal Whisperer

Shannon has always loved animals and worried about them. Her Dad and I took her to the circus when she was three and she worried the whole time about the animals. Where were their mothers? Where did they sleep? What did they eat? It was the beginning of a love affair.

As a married adult, she worked in veterinary clinics in Florida and Virginia. Not only did she continue to worry about animals but the homeless ones and the sick ones that nobody wanted, found a home with her and then husband, Drew, resulting in a domestic-animal zoo. Ferrets, sugar gliders, ducks, rabbits, dogs, cats, birds, plus other creatures who were recuperating before going back into the wild, were all fed and loved in her home.

There were also special missions. When the Animal Rescue facility wound

133

up with too many bunnies, they found a farm family in Kentucky who would adopt them. A 20-hour car ride later, Shannon and Drew released fifteen happy bunnies from their cages into grassy fields.

During one summer when Florida was hit by one hurricane after another, baby ducks were rescued and lived in their swimming pool for a while, moving to the guest room bathtub while one of the worst storms passed through. Can you imagine cleaning up after a bathtub visit of baby ducks? All survived and were returned to the outside world when they were old enough.

As years went by and Shannon stopped working in vet clinics, the stream of adoptees slowed. But there were always cats and dogs, each with a distinctive personality and often, names to match. There was Stinky (for obvious reasons) and Tortilla (Torti for short). There were twin sisters, Frances and Jean, raised from kittens and bottle fed because they had been discarded by their human family. Penny was a feral cat who was afraid of people and despite Shannon's best efforts, slept under the bed and only came out to roam at night. It was a major victory when Penny began coming out to share breakfast time and talk with Torti. Morris was a ginger cat, a massive ball of fur who slept where he wanted and ate when he chose.

They were all referred to as the kids and treated as such. Some came with disabilities that required operations or costly medications. Somehow, Shannon managed to provide what they needed, even when it meant ignoring her own needs. After her divorce, she met a kind, caring man, A. J., who loves her and her menagerie, and cheerfully shares the home and kid chores, giving her more time for her studies.

The furry kids have dwindled from a one-time high of eleven cats and dogs, down to three cats - Frances, Jean and Penny, and one dog, Daisy. Each time she loses one to disease or old age, she buries them in a tiny casket with their name on it, honors them with flowers, weeps over them, and remembers them, every single one.

A remarkable woman, my daughter.

Welcome To The World

When Steven and Shannon were born, I started a book for each of them, not cluttered with dates and statistics but filled with moments-joyous, funny, poignant, about their growing up years. I presented the handwritten books to them, along with a scrapbook of photos when they graduated from high school. When Steven and Amy told me I was going to be a grandmother, I was ecstatic and encouraged them to do something similar for their children. I gave them a blank book and this *welcome to the world* letter was the first contribution. When Emma and Zachary arrived, I delivered similar books, with a welcome letter in each. I'm happy they are maintaining the tradition.

Dearest Adaline,

Welcome to our family! You are a lucky little girl to be born to parents who love each other and adore you, plus grandparents, aunts, uncles and cousins who couldn't wait for your arrival.

Pop-pa and I were so excited to meet you in person. We had already oohed and aahed over your pictures and couldn't wait to hold you in our arms.

You have arrived into a world full of conflicts and prejudices. I hope as you grow up, you will become a person who can see people for who they are on the inside, rather than how they look on the outside. I hope you will be a protector of our land - - our mountains, rivers and skies - - as your Cherokee ancestors taught.

I wish for you a fun childhood with lots of time to play and dream. When you become an adult, I wish for you a career that you are passionate about, caring friends, and a soul mate, like I found in Pop-pa, who will love you unconditionally and hold your hand through lifes ups and downs. What wonderful adventures you have ahead of you! Live life to the fullest and always remember how much you are loved.

Gramma

Emma, Steven, Adaline, and Zachary

Fathers

Today I saw a toy truck and a love-worn doll,
and I thought of other places and other times.

I thought of a nine-year-old, tears streaming,
beating on his upstairs window with his small fists,
as his dad drove away from us, forever.

I thought of the days and nights,
and weeks and months, and years,
of anger and pain we all soldiered through.

I thought of the questions, without answers,
and cub scouts, and proms, and graduations,
without a father's hug or a father's pride.

As I looked at the yellow truck and the faded doll,
and the three squealing, giggling children,
climbing all over their adored Dad, I felt an old burden lift.

My son, Steven, who was that heart-broken nine-year-old,
had allowed his heart to heal,
and now it overflowed with love for his own family.

His grin from across the room
erased any lingering single Mom guilt.

His annual Father's Day cards to me
had been trying to do that for years.

I highly recommend grand-parenting. If you don't have any grandchildren of your own, borrow someone else's for a day. They change our perspective, ground us. It's hard to be tired or grumpy when a child is helping you rediscover buttercups and ant colonies. They take us back to our innocent beginnings. My grandchildren, Adaline, Emma and Zachary, live in a different state but today's digital miracles allow me to see them, talk to them and be an audience at their soccer games, school programs, even watch them learning to ride their bikes.

Steven and Amy share them with me every day. They are an endless source of entertainment.

Grandchildren Rock

They dance and they giggle,
give out lots of hugs.
They're wide-eyed at rainbows.
They even like bugs.

They're loving and trusting.
They're smarter than us.
If something's not perfect,
they say, "What's the fuss?"

They remind us of wonderful
years that are past,
when their parents were children
The time went so fast.

They're tomorrow on steroids,
these grandkids so bright.
We want to protect them,
make their lives right.

But each generation
must find it's own way.
We'll cheer from the sidelines,
as they brighten our day.

138

When I read story books to my grandchildren about fairies and magical places, I must admit I sometimes wish for one of those secret hideaways where I could escape all the complications and responsibilities of adulthood. One day, a friend took me on a tour of her springtime garden. Underneath the trees was a perfect ring of Lady Slippers. The only thing missing was fairies dancing in the moonlight.

My Secret Garden

I have a secret hiding place,
a spot untouched by time and space.

Its hidden underneath the trees,
and carpeted by last year's leaves.

My favorite time is in the spring,
when Lady Slippers form a ring.

The scent of damp moss is perfume,
that permeates my outdoor room.

Wild birds become my loyal pets,
and rest among the violets.

And when the moon is full and bright,
The fairies dance all through the night.

Don loved telling funny stories to our grandchildren.

One of his favorites was about the Easter Bunny, who he insisted, was really an Easter Frog. He convinced the kids it was the frog who delivered all the colored eggs and baskets. I wanted to keep some of those stories alive and pass them down to Zachary, the youngest, who didn't get to hear them from the master story-teller himself. This poem became an Easter card for them.

Easter Surprise

There once was a little green frog,
who lived in a woodsy bog.
Feeling lonely, one sunny day,
he decided to hip-hop away.

As he hopped 'neath the trees,
through the warm spring breeze,
he heard voices ahead.
"Sounds like fun!" he said.

He hopped and hopped with all his might,
and saw before him, a wondrous sight.

The grass was sprinkled with purple and blue,
and yellow and green and bright pink too.
He saw eggs of all colors, in baskets and bins
and bright colored water in saucers and tins.

He hopped in the water and jumped cup to cup.
He wriggled down in and then he jumped up.
His legs were purple, his mouth, bright blue.
His back was speckled with yellow goo.

The sun was toasty -- he needed a nap.
So he hopped in a basket -- zippity zap!

When the children returned from their hike to the bog,
they cheered, in surprise, "It's the Easter Frog!!"

Don Frew and Emma

As Steven grew into an adult, I wondered how the divorce and subsequent alienation from his Dad would affect his own relationships. I watched with admiration as he completed his Bachelor's Degree and then his Masters, all the while, holding down full time jobs.

Over the years, as I've watched him evolve into a loving son, husband and father, I have stopped worrying. I recently poured my pride into this Father's Day poem for him.

Good Sons Good Fathers

Today, fathers come in all sizes and types...
fat ones and slim ones and dads who smoke pipes.
Dads who are single and dads who are wed,
march off to work to keep families fed.
Stay-at-home dads cook, sweep, and clean.
Work-at-home dads stare at Mac screens.

The best dad of all is the kind you've become...
a renaissance dad who works hard but has fun.
A dad who can sit in the floor and play dolls,
or run down the soccer field, chasing white balls.
A husband, a partner who carries his share
of the cooking, the ironing, whatever is there.

You're a dad who wipes noses and rocks kids to sleep,
who loves with abandon, makes promises to keep.
You never complain, your gratitude shines
for all of life's blessings, all of the time.
Grandkids like mine deserve only the best.
You've already scored an A+ on this test.

Spending time with grandchildren in this age of technology highlights the stark difference between my childhood and theirs. Relating to them requires a willingness to upgrade basic modes of communication. Most of the time, I find the changes advantageous. I can see them, talk with them, even read them a bedtime story when they're miles away. But I have to admit, there are other times when I miss those simpler days.

Return To Childhood

Let's go back in time, pre PC or Mac,
to my childhood days. You won't have to pack.

Red Rover, Red Rover, hide and go seek.
Jump rope and hopscotch, and swims in the creek.

Barefoot in springtime, bugs in fruit jars.
Dress-up in Mom's clothes, dolls in the yard.

Hard candy and apples in each Christmas sock.
If you were bad, then you might find a rock.

Hot bread with butter, the snack before bed.
Chocolate milk promised, when stories are read.

Lights out at bedtime, all covers tucked in.
Dreams of adventures, when new day begins.

Your childhood's different. Your life's so complex.
To stay in touch, I must learn how to text.

Some things, however, stay always the same.
Grammas and grandkids share bonds that don't change.

A Dorsey Family Christmas

Back Row L to R: Shannon, A.J., Sharon, Steven
Front Row L to R: Amy, Zachary, Emma, and Adaline

Our Christmases, when Steven and Shannon were young, were always spent in West Virginia with my parents, my brothers and their families. When my father died, my mother remained in the house where we all grew up. It was small, with three bedrooms and as time raced on, there were lots of us to pile in for the big holiday. But it didn't matter. It was tradition to go home for Christmas.

Years went by. My children went off to lives and families of their own, and it became impossible to gather all of us and go to the mountains for the holidays. The year I decided it was time to make that Christmas break and have our own Dorsey Family Christmas, my Mom was devastated, even though both of my brothers and their families came and filled the family home. I was guilt-ridden and found myself cooking all the things she cooked, trying, I suppose, to duplicate the Christmas I had always known.

It took a couple of years for the kids and I to begin to establish our own traditions and absolve ourselves of guilt for deserting the Canfield Family Christmas. When Shannon moved to Florida, we spent a couple of Christmases there, decorating palm trees. We all flew to Kentucky one year to christen Steven and Amy's new home. I look forward each year to our Dorsey Family Christmas. We are carrying on many of my Mom's traditions -- too much food, too many presents, and holiday decorations on everything.

A Dorsey Family Christmas Is...

The sharp scent of pine and burnt cookies,
'cause I was fa-la-laing
along with Rod Stewart's holiday CD,
and didn't hear the oven buzzer.

One more trip to the attic,
in search of Grandma's very worn, handmade angel,
which always has the place of honor on the top of the tree.

A frantic top to bottom house search
for all the presents I bought in July on sale,
and hid in places nobody would think of looking,
including me.

The annual pilgrimage to the local production
of the Nutcracker,
even though all those fancy-dressed little girls
in the audience
make me wonder how my little girl
got to be forty something.

The Sunday School nativity,
with the determinedly stoic Joseph, the shy, blushing Mary,
and the Youth Choir humming
Away in a Manger in the background.

Addressing dozens of Christmas cards and shedding tears
for the crossed-off names of beloved friends
and family members we lost this year.

Googling, *how to thaw a turkey quickly*,
when I realize the bird's still frozen solid,
and it's way past time to go into the oven.

Accepting accolades for my delicious dinner,
cleaning up all the mess,
then discovering the salads are still in the frig.

Christmas is all these things but so much more.
It is the realization that nothing really matters,
except those familiar, much-loved faces
around the dinner table.

Chapter 6

Musings From The Edge Of Understanding

Hopeful Words

Our lives are built on hopeful words.
They take us to a different place.

As a child, words took me to places where mommies and daddies didn't yell, and children were heard, as well as seen. At night, under the covers, with my books and my flashlight, I traveled to places filled with loving laughter, and I found hope there.

At nineteen, when my husband of one month, was transferred to Korea for a year, love letters sustained me, those words promising the storybook life I had dreamed of as a child, hiding beneath those blankets.

As a single parent, overwhelmed by my husband's betrayal, and the responsibilities of raising two young children alone, I poured my frustrations and joys into journals that would, many years later, help my daughter through her own divorce. Powerful words—questioning, lamenting, healing—words that reassured her, "Yes, this stinks! But you will survive and life will be good again."

When my soul mate of twenty-five years was diagnosed with terminal cancer, the journals came out again, and I allowed the words to pour, diluting the anger, the terror, and finally, the grief, into poems and stories of the life we had created together. When I cleaned out Don's desk, I found a box containing every love letter, every card, every poem I had ever written for him. The scrawled sticky note on top said, simply, *Our Life*. Now, words are my tools once again, as I visualize and turn the page to the next chapter of my life.

Sharon Canfield Dorsey
Daughter of the Mountains - A Memoir

Going Home Again

I used to live in the cream colored house on the corner,
the one with the Williamsburg Blue shutters and door.
The rickety fence still leans,
evidence of abuse by multitudes of climbing,
standing and crawling-under neighborhood kids.

The Charlie Brown maple sapling I planted
is resplendent in autumn rust and now proudly full grown,
like my two children who put down roots
in the blue shuttered house,
and then ripped them up to go in search
of enlightenment, adventure and themselves.

The house wears its twenty-five years
of birthday parties, graduations, and Christmases
more lightly than I.

Those seasons resonate in every nook and cranny
of my heart, bones, and mind.
The laughter and tears flash through,
and are gone in a blink,
leaving a melancholy residue of faintly echoing voices,
leaving me feeling as if I, too,
need a fresh coat of Williamsburg Blue paint.

Life Is What Happens During The Pauses

When I was in my twenties, my husband, Buddy, became so addicted to television, he basically lived his real life during the commercials. We discussed finances during the breaks. We planned vacations during those pauses. As a parent, pauses were brief times to play with his young son and, later, a daughter.

Bizarre as it sounds, many of our friends were just like us. We would get together for potluck dinners, and the activities of the evening would be scheduled around the commercial breaks in the ball games, or the movies. The women would sit in the kitchen, and complain to each other. But it was the 1960's, and man was still master of the house. None of us confronted the actual perpetrators of this ridiculous system. Years into the marriage, my husband used a commercial break to inform me that he was leaving us for another woman. When I recovered from the shock, I wondered how he found enough time away from television to meet someone else, much less have an affair with her.

As time went on, I experienced many magical moments, not during commercial pauses, but during life's pauses.

...The butterfly-in-the-stomach pause between the doorbell ringing and opening the door to meet the blind date, Don, who would become the love of my life. He, by the way, hated television.

...The blinding-tear pause just before my beautiful daughter walked out to join her fiancé on her wedding day.

...The heart-over-flowing pause as my son placed my first grandchild in my arms.

There were also many moments when I wished I could actually push a pause button and stop the world.

...The time-stood-still pause when John F. Kennedy was shot and we all waited and prayed that he would live.

...The terrifying pause on 9/11 just before the Twin Towers fell, when life as we knew it was changed forever.

...The gut-wrenching pause at the bedroom door as a tearful hospice nurse said, "I'm so sorry, honey, he's gone."

I have concluded, it is the simple pauses between these larger life-altering events that keep us sane and moving on through the drama.

...The awe-inspiring pause as the sun drops into the sea on a deserted white sand beach.

...The triumphant pause at the crest of a mountain as we emerge from the trees to stand with heads in the clouds.

...The peaceful pause at the end of a hard day's work, when you know you've done your best.

But I think the pause that puts everything else in perspective is that expectant moment as you wait for a friend, a spouse, a child, to respond with, "I love you too."

The Cycle Of Life

As I begin to acknowledge the reality of the O word (O meaning old) as it relates to myself, I see life as that O, a circle, beginning as a blank page and ultimately, ending with that same blank page, the slate wiped clean.

When my mother died a few years ago, I helped to clear out her home. My brothers and I were born and raised there. My mother lived there for seventy years. The walls should scream with the laughter and tears of all those years. But they stand silent, antiseptically clean, waiting for the next chapter. All that happened there, between beginning and end, seems to have been neatly erased.

If all trace of us is erased at the end, what is the purpose of the middle of life between the beginning and ending? Think about this...we begin life dependent on others and most likely, we will end it dependent in some way. Most of us start our adult lives penniless and, too often, we end our story similarly.

- So, is the in-between meant to be a time to accumulate money and things?
- Is it a time to acquire knowledge and wisdom and are those two things the same?
- Is it a time to search for perfect love, the soul mate who will supposedly complete us?
- Do we find happiness and the meaning of life in all of these things or none of them?
- And what, if anything, do we leave behind?

I hear my mother's words coming out my mouth all the time. I notice my children repeating their step-father's sayings. I believe what is left behind is not what is accumulated or taught, but rather what is CAUGHT by those whose lives we touch, even briefly. And I believe, strongly, that happiness and meaning are not attained by reaching a goal or a destination, but rather, during the spiral of the journey.

Circle

I am perfection,
my curves rounded, pleasing,
my many faces fascinating, beguiling.

I am the earth, tiny and vulnerable, as seen from space.
I am the moon, shadowed in clouds and mystery
on a harvest night.
I am a rainbow-colored soap bubble, wobbling skyward, riding on the wind.
I am a cool, smooth coin, shamelessly trading myself
for labor and treasure.
I am your mother's iron skillet, sizzling with breakfast love.
I am a red balloon, the reality star of birthday celebrations.
I am a hula hoop, a twirling, undulating tease.
I am the golden ring that bonds two people in love.
I am the egg, waiting impatiently to be fertilized,
creating new life.
I am the restless spiral propelling humanity
through life's journey.

I am Alpha and Omega,
the beginning,
and the end.

For several years, after my father died and I got divorced, and before I met Don, my Mom and I spent a lot of time together. She came to Williamsburg and stayed with Steven and Shannon if I needed to go on business trips. As the kids got older and were in college, she traveled with me on a lot of those trips to Dallas and other places. Old disagreements and misunderstandings faded away with the years and we became friends. It was heart-breaking when her personality began to change, as she developed signs of dementia. I lost my friend long before I lost my mother.

Once Upon A Time...

Once upon a time gone by,
my Mom and I were best friends.
Now, my Mother sees me as the enemy
who steals her independence.

Once upon a sunshine time,
my Mom and I cruised the Caribbean together.
Now, my Mother has forgotten,
and insists that I've never taken her anywhere.

Once upon a companionable time,
my Mom and I shopped till we dropped.
Now, my brother and I are the checkbook police,
who cancel her forgotten orders.

Once upon a carefree time,
my Mom laughed a lot, at life and obstacles.
Now, my Mother is afraid
and doesn't want to leave her house.

Once upon a golden time,
my Mom loved life and us, her sons and daughter.
Now, my Mother is filled with unexplained rage
toward all of us.

Once upon a much too brief time,
my Mom faded away, leaving this stranger, my Mother.
Now, my Mother, the stranger, is also gone,
and I weep.

Identity Crisis

Mirror, mirror on the wall,
I am my mother, after all.

I look in the mirror and what do I see?
A face that is you, not a face that is me.
People keep telling me this is the case.
There's no denying, that is your Mom's face.

I also keep hearing your voice in my head,
I just can't escape. I am still being led.
The worst part is not your advice in my ear.
The worse part is what I discovered this year.

I'm doing it too--dumping all that advice,
on family and friends, without thinking twice.
They do the eye roll that I did to you.
I guess it is karma. I hate it too.

You were the family gardening guru.
All flowers bloomed and sparkled for you.
You gifted me often with such lovely plants,
which I promptly killed, blamed it on ants.

Now my home overflows with blooms everywhere.
I am convinced your green thumb is still there.
So Mom, hope you're happy. You'll live on forever.
For I've become you. It's a bond I can't sever.

Over The River And Through The Woods

Grandma Bessie Blaine Kuhl and Sharon Canfield
Cooking ramps outside.
Ramps are wild onions found in woods.

The gravel road was impossible, dusty, narrow, winding, with potholes big enough to swallow a tractor trailer truck. At least the road hadn't changed. I wondered what changes I would find in my grandparents' old house at the end of the road. I knew it was still there. I had checked with a relative who still lived in Pt. Pleasant, a small farming community on the banks of the Ohio River. I hadn't been to Pt. Pleasant since my grandmother died, twenty-six years ago. My grandfather had lived there alone for a few months, then had sold the house and acreage to move closer to town.

As I threaded my way through the pot holes, I could hear Grandma grumbling affectionately to Granddaddy about the god forsaken location, so far from town, shopping, and all the things she liked to do. She never let him forget that retiring to the country was his idea.

They built the house themselves, with the help of friends and relatives. They furnished it with all the things they had collected in their travels during Granddaddy's working years as a saw filer with a large construction company.

Grandma loved souvenirs and what-nots—dustibles, my children call them now. At Grandma's house, they perched on every table and window sill, atop starched, crocheted doilies that she turned out by the dozens. I don't think I ever say my grandmother sitting down without some kind of needlework in her hands. She taught me to crochet and embroider. During summer visits, she helped me to create pillowcases and scarves for my hope chest—that collection of household things that young women of the 40's and 50's were expected to stockpile for their wedding day.

She said when Granddaddy proposed, her own hope chest was full of wonderful things that she could proudly contribute to their first home together. I still have some of those first crude doilies we crafted together. I thought they were beautiful because Grandma told me they were.

Grandma also gave me my first cooking lessons. We concentrated on the important foods like lemon pie and pineapple upside down cake. We created salads too, macaroni and potato salads, and deviled eggs. I was allowed to mash the boiled egg yolks, mix in the mayonnaise and mustard, with a touch of vinegar for that just right, tart flavor. It was a proud day when Grandma decided I was old enough to chop the homemade pickles for the salads.

Frying the chicken was a different matter. Grandma always did that herself, dredging the chicken pieces in a pie pan filled with flour and secret seasonings that made her fried chicken renowned at all the family picnics. I never graduated to fried chicken, but I was allowed to mash the potatoes for Sunday dinner while Grandma made the gravy from the chicken scrapings in the big iron skillet. We would wear aprons she had embroidered for us, mine hanging to my ankles, and grin at each other over our cooking pots. I never eat lemon pie or fried chicken without missing her.

I was shaken out of my musings by a fork in the road that I didn't recall. I wondered if I'd missed a turn. The fork to the right looked new, with no potholes. The left fork looked untraveled, a bit forbidding, with masses of tangled wild roses and blackberry bushes tumbling into the road, narrowing the lanes on both sides.

I stopped, considering the two options. I remembered going blackberry picking with Granddaddy and coming home at sundown, stained and tired, but laden with buckets of blackberries. Grandma would freeze or can them for the winter. She would also bake delicious cobblers that we would eat with homemade vanilla ice cream.

Granddaddy always carried home armfuls of the fragrant pink roses, too, for he knew Grandma loved them. She would declare this year's crop of wild roses to be the prettiest ever, and we'd stuff them in vases, sniffing appreciatively as we placed them in all the rooms. When Grandma died, Granddaddy made sure her coffin was covered with roses.

Taking a deep breath, I chose the left fork and continued my tedious journey through the potholes. I was rewarded with a familiar landmark, the fishpond where Granddaddy fished on cool, fall evenings and the swamp where Grandma gathered cattails for her autumn flower arrangements. I was on the right road. As children, arriving for our summer visit, my brothers and I would get rowdy when we saw the fish ponds because we knew we were almost there. We'd forget about the long hours in the hot, cramped car when we realized that Grandma and Granddaddy's house was at the top of the next hill.

We knew Grandma would be sitting in the swing on the screened porch overlooking the driveway, fanning herself and watching for us, as excited as we were. She was always in her apron because she'd been cooking all day, cakes, pies, baked ham, salads, and homemade bread. Oh, and fudge. She knew we loved her chocolate and peanut butter fudge, full of walnuts from Granddaddy's trees.

She'd rip the apron off when she saw us round the curve at the top of the hill and hobble down the steps to meet us. Grandma had been crippled all her life from a childhood fall. But she never considered herself handicapped and managed to do everything that everybody else did.

Granddaddy would be in the apple orchard or in the yard, setting up the croquet set.

He was the family croquet and horseshoes champion. He loved having new victims to beat. He never let us win, just because we were children. When we did occasionally win a game, it was an occasion for much celebration.

If we came to visit in late summer, Granddaddy might be tending his corn pit. He'd dig a fire-pit in the ground and we'd roast ears of corn from his garden. We learned not to pig out completely on the fresh, sweet corn because we knew there would be watermelon later. He carried the melons from the field in early morning and put them in the root cellar where it was cool. They were sweet and juicy on hot summer evenings.

He would come running too, from wherever he was, his old straw hat in one hand and his snuff box in the other. Grandma always grumbled about his snuff dipping but I noticed when we went into town for groceries, she always brought him a new can. He'd grin and kiss her on the cheek. She'd blush like a young girl and say, "You old devil!" Granddaddy was living with my mother when he died at age 94 and he still enjoyed his snuff whenever she wasn't watching.

I rounded a blind curve in the road and slammed on the brakes. The narrow wooden bridge that always squeaked and rattled as we crossed the creek was gone, replaced by a steel structure twice its size. I looked ahead, expecting to see a crumbling old church that had been converted to a residence when I was a child. I used to come down the hill to play with a girl named Carol, who lived there with her grandparents. No one seemed to know what had happened to her mother. "Some kind of scandal," my grandmother always muttered darkly, then quickly changed the subject. We felt sorry for Carol, living in that dark, moldy, old church, so we'd invite her up to play when we came to Grandma's to visit. Years later, when I was in high school, Grandma told me she had run away. Nobody ever heard of her again, and I used to wonder what happened to her.

The church was gone without a trace. Not even a chimney stone was left to mark its passing. I stopped the car on the other side of the steel-beamed bridge and got out. I walked through the tall grass under the giant oaks where we used to have a tire swing. I could hear Carol's squeals when I pushed her too high in the swing and her grandmother's croaking admonition to, "Be careful, children!" I wondered if we'd recognize each other today, Carol and I, two middle-aged women. Did she have children, a husband, and a bright sun-filled home? I hoped so.

I ran my hand over the cool bark of the oak tree. How many life cycles had it seen? How many more would pass beneath its branches? It was comforting to think there would be others who would build swings there.

I got back in the car and sat for a long time, looking up the hill toward Grandma and Granddaddy's house. I knew it was just ahead, hidden by the wooded curve in the road. For a moment, the familiar anticipation filled me. I closed my eyes and saw the joy in their faces and felt their arms around me. Once again, I felt warm and secure and loved.

I started the engine, turned the car around and headed back across the steel bridge.

The Cousin Connection

It was the late fifties.
My teenage summers were unbearably boring,
except for visits to my cousins, Charlie and Sandy.
Sandy was a year younger, Charlie a year older.

Sandy had red hair and beautiful clothes
and lots of boyfriends.
It was like bees to honey, boys always buzzing around her.
I had ordinary brown hair and dime store clothes,
and Daddy wouldn't allow bees or buzzing.

Sandy would let me borrow her full skirts and crinolines.
Charlie would take us to juke box dances at the state park.
Charlie and I sometimes won the jitterbug contests.
I felt like Cinderella at the ball when he was my partner.

Then we all grew up.
Charlie got a job and a wife and a daughter.
I went to college on the other side of the country.
Sandy married her high school sweetheart
and moved away.
We lost touch and fifty years disappeared, as if a moment.

Three years ago, my mother died.
At her wake, a strange man wrapped his arms around me
and whispered, "Can you still jitterbug?"
I was Cinderella at the ball once more.

The cousin connection resumed, only to be severed again
when Charlie lost his brave battle with cancer.
His passing reminded me that we, ourselves,
are diminished, when a someone who loved us
and has shared a chapter of our lives, is gone.

That chapter is now closed
and I will miss being Cinderella at the ball.

Elvis And Me

A long time ago,
I grew up in the house on the hill,
with the creaking porch swing
and the now-dark windows.

Elvis and I sang duets in that swing,
rockin' songs of Blue Suede Shoes
and Hound Dogs and tender ballads
promising love everlasting.

Daddy complained of the noise.
Mom didn't understand the lyrics.
Both predicted my rapid descent into hell
for memorizing the words from those evil 45's.

I have returned to the dark, silent house
hoping to channel that resilient sixteen-year-old
who was sure life would be an adventure,
sure she knew everything about everything.

Life and time, those slayers of dreams
and betrayers of promises,
worked their sinister magic
on Elvis and me.

Mom and Daddy are both gone,
taking with them their dire predictions
of eternal damnation.
Elvis deserted me in a hailstorm of uppers and downers,
and love everlasting, wasn't.

Wiping away grime and dust,
I settle into the rickety wooden slats,
activate the rusty chains,
and swing into a still defiant rendition of Jailhouse Rock.

Hate V. Love

On June 25, 2015,
the White House was illuminated in rainbow colors,
celebrating the Supreme Court decision,
affirming love.
A year later, the flag flies at half mast,
and the faces of forty-nine people
stare back at us from television screens--
murdered victims of hate.

What happened to love?
What happened to justice and the legal promise
that lesbian, gay, bi-sexual, and transgendered people,
could marry, care for their partners and children,
live as first class citizens,
in the land of the free and home of the brave?

Where does hate live?
It lives in churches who decline to unite gay couples,
in politicians who use fear of difference for personal gain,
in adoption agencies who refuse good parents
because of their sexual orientation,
in schools that deny bathroom privileges
to transgendered students,
in the hearts of people who scatter blame
on entire groups of people,
instead of on the perpetrators of the crimes.
It lives in every person who promotes or ignores
prejudice and discrimination.

How do we win the battle of Hate V. Love?
We stand together for justice,
fight prejudice with tolerance,
and love unconditionally.

Other Nations

Chickadees skitter across the half-frozen snow,
wings fluttering, beaks chipping at the ice.

My young children used to ask me
why their feet didn't freeze.
My daughter tried to make bird boots
out of old leather gloves.

I told them that Mother Nature protects and provides.
They were satisfied, but I wasn't, quite.

How do they know to fly before the hurricane arrives?
Who tells them when it's time to migrate in the fall?
What's the clue that it's safe to return in the spring?
And who chooses the lead bird in the V formation?

My very wise husband summed up
the mystery best.
They have senses that we have never had
or have long forgotten.

They are not underlings.
They are not equals.
They are other nations.

The Human Race

Election night, 2003.
Glued to my television, as state after state
come in for Barrack Obama.
Envying the crowds in Grant Park, cheering, hugging.

Inauguration Day, 2004.
Cameras focus on faces in the audience,
black, white, brown, yellow,
united across ethnic and racial barriers by joy, amazement.

Flashback ...High school, 1958.
Beginnings of integration in my small coal mining hometown in West
Virginia -- the same unity of spirit,
but this time, motivated by grief, not joy.
Our high school was integrated that year with little fanfare.
The new students weren't mistreated,
just ignored and whispered about at lunchtime,
neither group willing to make that first inclusive move.

Then tragedy struck.
Three black children, playing beside a flood-swollen creek, fell into the
swirling water.
Despite attempts to reach them,
the fast-moving waters carried them away.
Word spread quickly.
People rushed to the creek and waded in to search.
Hours passed and darkness descended.
Then a man waded out, carrying a small body,
his cheeks wet with tears.

Within an hour, two more small bodies
joined the first on the creek bank.
As we gathered around the agonized family,
we learned the father was unemployed.
Their five children had been taking turns
going to school for lack of clothes and shoes.
Suddenly, racial differences were swept aside.
The next day, donations of food, clothing, and money
were ferried across the flooded creek in rowboats.

The service for the children was held
in our high school gymnasium,
the only building large enough to hold all those
who wanted to show their respect.
It was strange at that time to see
black and white people sitting side by side.

At the end of the service,
a dignified black woman walked to the front of the room.
She spoke words I have never forgotten.
"You have made us feel today that there is only one race,
and that is the human race."

How much longer will it be
before those words become truth?

Homer Dale Canfield

Elegy For Homer

White hair frames a drawn, weary face on the pillow.
How did my laughing little brother
become this aged, dying man?
Where had the time gone?

I close my eyes and see him running through the grass
in his cowboy hat and boots, shooting invisible villains
with his toy rifle or bow and arrows,
our younger brother, Carl, trailing in his footsteps.

He would grow up and learn to shoot a real rifle
as a member of the Air National Guard,
and he would hunt deer with real bow and arrows
in the West Virginia mountains.

As his life ebbs away before my eyes,
I hope his last memories are as vivid as mine,
of childhood Easter egg hunts, snowy Christmases,
family camping trips, and boisterous birthdays.

As he travels through the kaleidoscope of his adult life,
I wish him only happy memories --
of family weddings, his, Carl's, and mine;
of our children, playing, growing up together;
and as he moves on through the years,
of his grandson, his pride and joy.

As his eyes close and he passes into that unknown world,
I hope Mom and Daddy and all of the ancestors
are waiting to welcome him into a world without pain,
without sadness.
I kiss his forehead one last time and wish him peace.

1945 - 2015

I Have Always Wondered...why bad things happen to good people.

Why do children get cancer? Why does one soldier die from enemy gunfire, and the soldier standing next to him survive? Why are entire cities wiped out by natural disasters? Why does only one person walk away from a plane crash? Why would a loving God allow these things to happen?

From an early age, I declared myself a seeker of truth. I thought, if I read enough, if I learn enough, I will find the answer to that troubling question. There have been times when I thought I was close to the answer. When I studied reincarnation, it made sense to me that perhaps we have lived many times before. That would explain the feeling of familiarity I sometimes feel, meeting someone for the first time; or the shiver that went down my spine when I walked into a castle in Britain, and knew where everything was before the tour guide told me.

I related to the Buddhist view of karma: that what you put out in the world, good or bad, comes back to you. Were bad things happening to people as punishment for bad things they had done in a previous life? I liked the idea that when we die, our souls rest between lives, and we choose our next life for the lessons we need to learn. I rationalized, if we know ahead of time what to expect, and we still choose that life, God isn't making bad things happen. He is simply allowing us free will.

When my husband was diagnosed with terminal cancer, he was very pragmatic about dying. When I voiced my anguish by asking, "Why you?", his response was, "Why NOT me? We are all going to die. I just happen to know approximately when and from what."

As we went through that last year, I kept going back to that idea of karma, searching for acceptance of this awful thing that was happening. Had Don chosen this life knowing he would survive Vietnam, only to die of a cancer he got from the chemicals he inhaled there? What lessons could he possibly have learned from all that? He would have called all of my speculations juju. He believed we are no different from the plants and animals: we live, we die, and that's it. Nothing stays behind or returns. So I am left with that question, "Why DO bad things happen to good people?"

And for now, my answer is, "I still don't know." But they do happen, so hopefully, the lessons we learn from those bad things will make us more tolerant people—perhaps moving us toward that ultimate goal of my own personal brand of religion: think kind thoughts, do kind deeds, and love one another unconditionally.

Nirvana

Pay attention...to black earth, yielding life.

...to sun's warmth on bare skin.

...to lotus blossoms, rising.

...to ants, working beneath your feet.

...to your neighbor's pain.

...to love, freely given.

...to the wonder of your breath.

Pay attention...to attain enlightenment.

Then let it all go.

Summer's Swan Song

The browning grass begs one last mowing.
The grocery list languishes on the kitchen table.
The car needs serious cleaning.

But scarlet leaves dance on a playful breeze,
the final chapter of my summer book waits expectantly,
and a languid sun envelops me in its seductive blanket.

My lounge chair on the porch beckons.
Bolstered by a sweating glass of sweet tea with lime,
I eagerly surrender to summer's swan song.

Chapter 7

My Seventies Rebellion

Seventy!!!!!!

My 70th birthday came and went with no celebration. On that day, my husband Don was admitted to the hospital in critical condition. His rare form of bone marrow cancer had morphed into acute leukemia, and there were no more treatment options, just as our doctor had predicted. Since the beginning diagnosis, we had asked for truth, so he pulled no punches now: Don had a week, maybe two.

The three of us, Don, Shannon, and I, looked at each other and didn't know what to say. It wasn't a surprise but yet, it was, because we each had hoped for a miracle. Don broke the tearful silence, "Guess we'll just have to have a two-week party." It was so ludicrous, we were all suddenly laughing, crying, and creating ridiculous funeral scenarios involving the solemn Arlington Cemetery funeral parade, complete with caisson and band but led by Don's favorite troupe of belly dancers. I know-crazy! But it got us through those first awful moments of trying to deal with what lay ahead.

Needless to say, the belly dancers never made their debut at Arlington Cemetery. As a matter of fact, after a year of planning with Arlington—because that seemed a fitting resting place for a veteran with 31 years of service—we canceled those arrangements, and went with what Don really wanted: a parade of kayaks, placing his ashes in a quiet stream behind his best friend's house, and a rose from me, floating on the water. A song—*Take Me to the River*—written by a kayaking buddy, played in the background, and a family of eagles watched from their nest in the trees across the creek. We all knew, somewhere, he was smiling.

We were all smiling, too. Through our tears, we told funny stories, hugged each other, and reminded ourselves of Don's wishes that his memorial be filled with laughter.

It wasn't so easy to laugh in the weeks that followed his death. After fifteen months as Don's care-giver and twenty-five years as his constant companion, the hole in my life was cavernous. I was still working as a *Mary Kay* Sales Director, and my family of beauty consultants was a strong support system. It merged with the reinforcement from my children and close friends. Somehow, every day, I managed to get up, do what needed to be done as those first weeks and months passed. I missed Don every day. I still do.

I saw a plaque during those early months, that said, "The greatest gift we can give to those who have left us, is to live fully in their place." I made a conscious choice to do that. I started taking some classes through the *College of William and Mary,* just for fun. I was fortunate to be invited to join a poetry group, the *James City Poets*, and discovered a circle of talented new friends. I met a wonderful publisher who liked my work and published my first poetry book, *Tapestry,* in 2016.

Years earlier, on one of our trips to Cooper Island in the British Virgin Islands, I had written a children's story about a mysterious experience Don and I had with a large group of hermit crabs. That story, *Herman, the Hermit Crab, and the Mystery of the Big, Black, Shiny Thing,* became a picture book, with the help of my artist friend, Vivien. It was also published in 2016, and dedicated to my grandchildren.

This memoir, *Daughter of the Mountains*, completes the 2016 trilogy. But there are lots more stories and poems in my head, waiting to be written. I wake up every morning, curious about the experiences the new day might bring, hoping I can continue to write about them, and more importantly, laugh about them.

A Tribute To The Creaky Knee Brigade

At 20, I thought 50 was old.
At 40, I thought 70 was ancient.
At 70, I still feel 50, except for the creaky knees,
aching back and the way I look in the mirror.
Who is that woman?

Oh yeah, there's also the forgetfulness thing.
I can name and describe all my friends from high school.
I remember the names of all the rock stars of the 60's.
Yesterday, I couldn't recall my best friend's husband.
The name popped in, but hours later when it didn't matter,
like an obsolete computer in slooow mo.

So far, I haven't found my lost keys in the refrigerator
but I do sometimes go downstairs to get something,
and forget what that something is, which makes me think our brain must be
located in our butt.
As soon as I return to the scene and sit down, I remember.

Sometimes, I find myself wishing for simpler days,
when tiny gadgets didn't rule our world,
when people answered their phones and talked to me,
when I was a size 8 and sexy,
when my children were young and I could hug them daily,
when I felt safe in movie theaters and airplanes.

I am determined not to go quietly into that good night.
Brain foods, wrinkle creams, and Silver Sneakers at the Y,
I'm your girl, hereby declaring war on the O word,
refusing to go down without a fight.
Now, if I can just find those keys,
and remember where I was going...

Super Girl

Saw a flock of geese today,
looking tiny, far away.
Wondered how they keep that V,
choose who the lead bird will be.

Experts say it isn't easy,
'specially when the weather's breezy.
V formation lets them ride
on the up-draft by their side.

Saving energy and power,
keeping them aloft for hours.
Quite a feat, migrating geese
fly like jets and keep the V.

Makes me wish I, too, could fly
without jet, into the sky.
Super Girl in skirt and cape.
Watch me go. Just let them gape.

Remember When...

A trip on a plane was a really big thing.
We dressed in our best, chose a seat by the wing.
A stewardess served drinks, and then we had lunch,
and later, she brought us more peanuts to crunch.

The pillows were free, the blankets were soft.
The pilot told stories while we were aloft.
And when we arrived at our prime destination,
our luggage was there. We could start our vacation.

What happened? What happened? That is the cry.
Can't get on the plane 'till they're sure we don't lie.
Search luggage and shoes and all body parts.
Do pat-downs and x-rays before the trip starts.

Terrorists' bombs sewn in men's underpants.
Half-crazy passengers screaming out rants.
No food are we given without cash to pay.
No promise we'll even arrive the same day.

Flights cancelled, postponed, and sadly, some lost.
Whatever disaster, stay cool, at all cost.
Don't argue or mutter or utter complaints.
They'll wrap you in acres of *Duck Tape* restraints.

I've now removed flying from my favorite things,
I just get on, hoping the plane has two wings.

Wish I Knew...

...where the Land of Lost Dryer Socks is located.

...why I feel 50 on the inside and look 70 on the outside.

...why a dinner of mac and cheese is so much more
comforting than a dinner of broccoli.

...why my neighbor's chickens use my sidewalk
for a bathroom instead of the grass.

...what awful thing I did to deserve a neighbor
with chickens.

...why it's easy to remember events from fifty years ago
and so hard to recall what I did last week.

...who chooses ordinary names like Mary and John
for Customer Service operators with obvious
foreign accents. Do they really think we won't notice?

...why other people think they have perfect grandchildren,
when I am the Gramma who really does.

...why my hair looks its worst on photo day
and its best on hair-cut day.

...why I wonder about so many silly things.

This Is War

I am today declaring war,
and I intend to even scores
with service agents, far and near
who've left me holding, all this year.

Their placating patter does not soothe my ire.
It makes me, instead, more determined to fire
each one with the nerve to once more calmly say,
"Please hold," when we both know
they're gone for the day.

"Your call is important," is their favorite rap.
I want to respond, "No, it's not, you big sap."
"Be back in a minute," I hear all the time.
I want to yell back, "I will soon lose my mind."

But I hold and I wait, and I sputter and fuss,
I'd much rather throw things and hang up and cuss.
When a real person finally comes on the line,
I swallow it all and reply, "Yes, I'm fine."

But I am today declaring war,
and I intend to even those scores.
Now, when they return with promises bold,
They'll hear my recording, "Gone out. Please hold."

The
Bluebird
Of Happiness

I think I must be obsolete.
I still prefer talking to texting
I don't speak emoji.
I'd rather shop in stores than online.
I request real gifts, instead of gift cards.
I want to confer with my doctor face to face,
not on my I-pad.
I like my furniture already assembled.
I refuse to attend a funeral viewing drive-thru.
I like real grass, bugs and all.
I think families should spend Thanksgiving together,
not waiting in endless lines for *ToysRUs* to open.
I feel it's wrong for parents to tell kids there is no Santa.
Of course there is. I have the January bills to prove it.
Just when I think I'm adjusting to the new tech innovations,
and I'm going to be
the cool Gramma,
I get the cruelest news of all...
the bluebird of happiness is now a drone.

I'm Over All That

I'm over high heels that pinch,
and tight belts that cinch.

I don't care what's trending
or what tweets you're sending.

I banned books on weight loss,
and bought one on cheese sauce.

This confession's the worst.
I eat my dessert first.

I write poems in my pj's,
avoid restaurants with DJ's.

I declared war on phonies,
and all their baloney.

I think age is a mind game,
a tiger we CAN tame.

I'm ignoring that cat,
'cause I'm over all that.

It Is A Very Good Year

When I was 17, it was a very good year.
It was a very good year for football games
and walks, hand in hand.
Graduation arrived. I wondered what lay ahead,
when I was 17.

When I was 21, it was a very good year.
It was a very good year for feeling grown up
and tackling the world.
We searched for careers. We had married our loves,
when we were 21.

When I was 25, it was a very good year.
It was a very good year for married life
and babies who cried.
We bought homes of our own, and worked hard, 9 to 5,
when we were 25.

When I was 35, it was a very strange year.
It was a very strange year for family life
and marriage and trust.
My husband announced...our marriage would end,
when I was 35.

When I was 45, it was a very good year.
It was a very good year for kids growing up
and life going on.
It was a challenging time. Then a new love arrived,
when I was 45.

When I was 55, it was a very good year.
It was a very good year for hitting the road
and living our dreams.
We could follow the sun. We could live the good life,
when I was 55.

When I was 65, it was a very good year.
It was a very good year for settling down
in our gorgeous new house.
We still followed the sun but we loved coming home,
when I was 65.

And now I'm 70+ and it's a very good year.
It's a very good year for applauding good health
and a brain that still works.
Grandkids are a gift, to be treasured and loved,
now that I'm 70+.

As I am writing this book and remembering the past,
I lift my glass to all those growing up years
that rushed by me so fast.
I wouldn't want to go back. I'm still growing up.

This is a very good year.

About the Cover

Sharon Dorsey commissioned artist, Vivien Mann, to create the cover. She wanted to combine the spirit of her Cherokee ancestors with the essence of the mountains -- it's emerald green forests, sapphire skies, and crystal clear streams.

The result was "Spirit Guide."

Vivien Mann is a mixed media artist and has exhibited her work in Arizona and Virginia. She enjoys painting, jewelry making and recycling "found" objects into interesting new creations.

She is the mother of two children, Jenna and Matthew and several furry friends. She illustrated *Herman the Hermit Crab and the Mystery of the Big, Black, Shiny Thing* and created the cover for *Tapestry*.

About the Author

Sharon Dorsey is a member of the James City Poets and has received awards from the Poetry Society of Virginia, Chesapeake Bay Writers and Christopher Newport University Writer's Conference.

Her work has been published in magazines, journals, and anthologies. She has two children, Steven and Shannon, and three grandchildren, Adaline, Emma, and Zachary.

Other books by Sharon Canfield Dorsey

Hermit the Hermit Crab, and the Mystery of the Big, Black, Shiny Thing

Tapestry - Poems by Sharon Canfield Dorsey